BASIC
GETTING STARTED

WILLIAM S. DAVIS   MIAMI UNIVERSITY

▲ ADDISON-WESLEY PUBLISHING COMPANY

Reading, Massachusetts □ Menlo Park, California
London □ Amsterdam □ Don Mills, Ontario □ Sydney

D1295620

Library of Congress Cataloging in Publication Data

Davis, William S.   1943-
   BASIC – – getting started.

   1. Basic (Computer program language) I. Title.
QA76.73.B3D38   001.64'24   80-24868
ISBN 0-201-03258-9

ISBN 0-201-03258-9
   EFGHIJ-AL-89876543

Preface

The fact that you are reading this book indicates that you would like to learn to write computer programs. Perhaps you envision a professional career. You may need a tool to support your research. Your major department may require a programming course. Do you own a personal computer? If so, playing games designed by someone else may be losing its appeal. It could be that you are just curious, and want to learn more about these machines. The reasons are many.

If you want to learn how to program, you must begin somewhere. The intent of this book is simple: to help you get started. It is likely that the most difficult program you will ever write will be your very first one. Our objective is to guide you step-by-step through your first few programs until you are "over the hump" and feel comfortable with the machine.

There is an axiom in the computer field: The only way to learn to program *is* to program. We subscribe to that axiom. Once you have mastered the basics, the only way to improve your skill will be to write more programs. That is up to you.

But what does "to program" mean? Beginners often assume that programming is simply writing instructions in a programming language. A program is a series of instructions much as a novel is a series of sentences; syntax, spelling, and grammer are important, but there is more to the novel—and the program! The beginner who misses this essential point often becomes so bogged down in rules and syntax, that nothing is accomplished. The student knows how to write a valid instruction, but does not know what instruction to write next.

A program *is* a series of instructions. More accurately, it's a series of instructions designed to tell the computer how to perform some function, such as how to compute an average, or how to compute payroll, or how to sort data into sequence. The computer has no intelligence of its own. The programmer supplies that intelligence by telling the computer *exactly* (and we do mean exactly) what to do. Before the programmer can tell the computer how to solve a problem, he or she must know how to solve that problem. The first step in the program development process is therefore a logical one: solve the problem, using such tools as intelligence, logic, mathematics, and common sense. Only when the problem has been solved should the programmer begin the largely mechanical process of translating that solution into a programming language.

In writing a program, the programmer must be able to answer two questions:

1. What instruction should I code next?

2. How do I code that instruction?

To answer the first question requires logic. Reference manuals are written to answer the second question, explaining (in detail) how to code a specific instruction in a specific language. In other words, you can look up the answer to the second question, almost mechanically. Professional programmers, of course, understand the dual nature of the programming task. A few beginners seem to grasp this idea intuitively. Many do not. Without a plan to provide a context, programming seems an almost magical art—try something and see if it works. Discouraged, many quit before they actually begin. Usually, the problem is not a lack of aptitude or ability; often, the beginner has simply not grasped what "to program" means.

And so, we return to our objective: helping you get started. We begin by developing a solution to a problem, without referring to any language. In Chapter 2, this solution is translated into BASIC and submitted to the computer, with each step clearly described. As your skill (and confidence) increases, you should have little trouble with the more complex problems that are solved and coded in subsequent chapters.

There is a standard for minimal BASIC. Most versions of BASIC go beyond this standard, and there are significant differences between the versions of BASIC offered by the various manufacturers. We have tried to stay within the minimal standard. The programs in this text were run on a Hewlett-Packard 3000, series II computer system, but should run with little or no modification on almost any computer. It is not our intent to cover every feature of BASIC. Our goal is to help you get started. Ideally, after reading this book and writing a few programs, you will be able to read the BASIC reference manual and discover new features for yourself. If so, we will have achieved our objective.

WSD
Oxford, Ohio

Contents

to

Carl and Jay

Defining
and Planning
a Problem Solution

1

OVERVIEW

In this chapter, we will follow, step-by-step, the process of developing a solution to a problem suitable for submitting to a computer. The problem we've chosen is very general: computing an average. We'll begin by carefully defining the problem to be solved. Next, we'll structure a human-level solution, using such generally accepted and understood everyday tools as a pocket calculator and a counter. Having specified a fairly complete human-level solution, we'll briefly discuss a few elementary computer concepts and then restructure our solution to fit the requirements of these machines, developing a flowchart and a description of the data to be processed. Once these tasks have been completed, we'll be ready to begin coding the program in BASIC.

A CAUTIONARY NOTE BEFORE WE BEGIN

Computers are fascinating machines. But they are just machines, capable of doing nothing without detailed instructions provided by some human being. Because you are reading this book, you are probably interested in learning how to write these detailed sets of instructions, called programs. You must remember, however, that the computer can do *nothing* that you yourself do not know how to do. In other words, the responsibility for solving the problem is yours, and not the computer's. Yes, the computer is very accurate, but "accuracy" may not mean exactly what you think. Computers are considered accurate because the results they generate are highly predictable. If you tell a computer to add 2 and 2, it will invariably get 4. If the programmer didn't really mean to have the computer add 2 and 2, it will *still* get 4. The wrong instructions will produce the wrong answer with perfect "accuracy".

A computer is programmed in a programming language; the language we've chosen for this text is BASIC. Anyone can learn to write instructions in BASIC—it's just a matter of practice. There is, however, much more to programming. Before a problem solution can be coded in any language, there must be a problem solution. The primary purpose of this book is to show you how to develop such solutions. We'll be using a very methodical, structured approach, the top-down approach, to program development. As you begin to learn more about programming, the temptation will be to skip planning and careful preparation, and immediately begin coding a solution. Don't. As your skill increases, you will find yourself attempting more and more difficult problems, so the need for careful planning *never* disappears. *Think!* Then do.

DEFINING THE PROBLEM

Let's start with a very common problem: computing an average. Undoubtably, you have computed your grade point average, your batting average, your freethrow percentage, or some other average. What does it mean to compute an average? If you had to perform this task, what would you do?

Your view of the problem is probably going to be shaded somewhat by your background. If you are a mathematician, your basic definition of this problem is simply

$$\overline{X} = \frac{\sum\limits_{i=1}^{n} X_i}{n}$$

For many people, the mathematical definition isn't very useful. Perhaps, your view of the problem consists of the following two steps:

1. add together all the values you wish to average,

2. divide by the total number of values.

The result, in either case, will be an arithmetic average (or mean).

In technical terms, we have just defined an **algorithm**, a set of rules which, if followed precisely, will lead to a correct solution. Note that both the mathematical version and the English language version are valid algorithms; the use of mathematical conventions is *not* essential.

We now know, in very general terms, what has to be done. The question that remains is, "How do we do it?". Let's move along to the planning stage, where we will attempt to answer that question.

PLANNING A MANUAL SOLUTION

If you had to compute an average, precisely how would you go about it? We've already developed an algorithm; looking at that list of two steps, you might feel mildly insulted by the question. It seems obvious. Just

      1. add all the values,

      2. divide by the number of values.

It *is* obvious. You are, after all, a human being. Having stated the algorithm, you know how to solve the problem.

True. But that doesn't help us bring the problem solution down to the computer's level. We must be more precise. A useful technique for introducing this added detail is to set up a straw person. Assume that this person is unbelievably dense, and is capable of doing only what he or she is told to do. Instructions must be in the form of simple sentences—one verb. Each instruction must specify one and only one very specific action; this person literally cannot chew gum and walk at the same time. Now, tell this person how to compute an average. (You might even get your roommate to play the role.)

We might add a bit of structure to this technique by giving our straw person a pocket calculator (after all, everyone has a pocket calculator). We are now ready to begin instructing this imaginary individual as to exactly how to go about computing an arithmetic average.

What's wrong with simply saying, "Add all the numbers together"? How many numbers are there? If we assume there are 50 numbers, we are asking our straw person to do 50 things. The limit is 1! Our imaginary person can do only 1 thing at a time. We must be more precise.

Breaking this part of the problem into individual steps might produce the following list:

      1. Enter the first number.

      2. Push the ADD button.

      3. Enter the second number.

4. Push the ADD button.

5. Enter the third number.

6. Push the ADD button, and so on.

The pattern should be obvious. Note that each instruction is a simple sentence telling the straw person to perform one and only one very specific function.

How many instructions would we need? If we wanted to find the average of 50 numbers, we would need 50 "Enters" and 50 "Adds". One thousand numbers would require 1000 sets of instructions. Defining a solution in this way would become tedious. Chances are, you would consider taking a shortcut. Consider, for example, the following:

1. Enter a number.

2. Push the ADD button.

3. Are there any more numbers?

4. If yes, go back to step 1.

How many numbers would this little block of logic add together? How many numbers do we have? Our straw person, following these four instructions, would accumulate values until there were no more values to accumulate. In programming terminology, we'd call this a **loop**.

We might try this logic just to see if, in fact, it works. Take a handful of numbers: 3 + 5 + 2 for example. We know that the correct sum is 10. Let's see if our logic produces that sum. Pick up your pocket calculator and do exactly what the instructions say. Don't clear it; where did you read an instruction that says "Clear the calculator"? Now add 3 + 5 + 2 and get 1347 or some other equally ridiculous answer. Why didn't your logic work? Obviously because you forgot to clear your calculator. By actually trying your solution, you are going through a process known as **desk checking**. It is an invaluable step. No matter how well you think you know what you are doing, there are always going to be little details that you will overlook. The only sure way to catch these oversights is by actually trying your logic. In fact, try it twice; the calculator just might have been cleared by the previous user and you might have missed this problem completely.

Adding the initialization step leads to the following five steps:

1. Clear calculator.

2. Enter a number.

3. Push the ADD button.

4. Are there any more numbers?

5. If yes, go back to step 2.

Now, desk checking should clearly indicate that if we follow the instructions "to the letter" we will successfully add any number of values.

What next? What do we do after there are no more numbers? It's time to divide the accumulated sum of values by the number of values to get the average. We might add step 6, as follows:

6. Divide sum by number of values to get average.

There is only one problem. We know the sum, but how many values were there? Before computing the average, we must count the values. Basically, we have two choices. We can go through our list of values all over again, this time counting instead of accumulating, or we can count values as we go along. The first choice might be reasonable if we have only a few values to average. If we are dealing with hundreds of data points, however, it makes sense to count as we go along. You might imagine yourself making a mark on a paper after adding each number to the accumulator, as in (ℍℍ ℍℍ llll), or you might use a mechanical counter. Our developing solution now becomes:

1. Clear calculator.

2. Set counter to zero.

3. Enter a number.

4. Push the ADD button.

5. Add 1 to counter.

6. Are there any more numbers?

7. If yes, go back to step 3.

8. Divide accumulator by counter to get average.

9. Copy average onto a sheet of paper.

That last step was added to make certain that a copy of the answer is saved.

We now have a pretty complete average program. The logic should work; desk check it with three or four values to be sure. Try it out on a classmate. Without describing the objective of the program, simply read the instructions, one at a time, and have your friend do exactly what you say. If the answer turns out to be correct, you will *know* that your program works.

Up to this point our objective was simply to define a problem solution in sufficient detail so that we can actually say that we know how to solve the problem. Now

5

that we know what to do, we can begin to discuss how we might adapt this solution to the computer. Before doing this, we must discuss a few very basic computer concepts.

THE COMPUTER

What exactly is a **computer**? Perhaps the best way to answer that question, without getting into unnecessary details, is to compare a computer to its first cousin, the calculator. Imagine actually implementing the problem solution described above on a calculator. Each time the instruction said "Enter a number," you would key in the value and press the "ENTER" button. Each time the instruction said "Push the ADD button," you would press the "ADD" or "+" button. Each step requires you, the human being, to decide what button is to be pressed, and then to press it. The precise steps may be a bit different with a different calculator, but the basic idea of the need for human participation at each and every step is still valid.

Imagine that you have a special machine that automatically pushes the proper buttons in the proper sequence. Given such a machine, calculations could be performed without human intervention. We'd have an automatic calculator. Of course, all the steps would have to be carefully thought out and "programmed" ahead of time, but if a particular set of computations had to be performed over and over again, many many times, the task of preparing the program would be worth the cost. Such an automatic calculator would be, essentially, a computer.

The basic difference between a computer and a calculator is that a computer is designed to function automatically, under control of a **program**, while a calculator is designed to require step by step human intervention. Basically, a computer is composed of two primary components (Fig. 1.1), a processor and memory. Programs are stored in the computer's memory. The processor performs two basic functions. First, it fetches a single instruction from memory and decodes the instruction, figuring out which specific operation is to be performed; this function is carried out by the control unit portion of the processing unit. Once the control unit has figured out what must be done, it turns control over to an arithmetic and logical unit (Fig. 1.1 again), which does what the instruction says to do. The same thing happens on a calculator, only you provide the control. At some point, you must decide which button to push, thus performing the function of the control unit. When you make up your mind, you push the button, and the calculator performs the function of the arithmetic and logical unit.

A computer is capable of executing a very limited set of instructions. Most computers can:

      1. add two numbers,

      2. subtract one number from another,

      3. multiply two numbers,

      4. divide one number into another,

Fig. 1.1: *The primary components of a computer.*

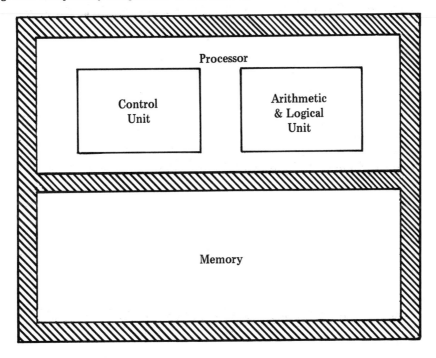

5. copy data from one memory location to another,

6. perform simple yes/no logic,

7. request the input of some data,

8. request the output of some data.

That's about it. A computer program is nothing more than a series of these very simple operations. Of course, they had better be the right operations, and they had better be in the right sequence, but basically that's all a program is.

A few of the computer's instructions need a bit more explanation. Addition, subtraction, multiplication, and division are obvious, so no additional detail is needed, but what is the copy function? Computers are not restricted to numeric data; they can process letters of the alphabet, punctuation marks, and numerous other forms of data as well. Imagine rearranging your laboratory notes into attractive tables and well-spaced prose. The computer, acting under control of the copy or "move" instruction, can do much the same thing, preparing attractive, well-spaced computer printouts.

What about the computer's yes/no logic capability? Look back at our human-level solution to the average problem. In step 6, we asked, "Are there any more numbers?" Step 7 said, "If yes, go back to step 2". That's yes/no logic. The computer can do much the same thing, checking to see if one number is bigger than another or if one letter comes before another in the alphabet. As we get into the BASIC language, we'll begin to discover just how powerful this skill really is.

Input and output may well be new concepts to many of you. Let's once again return to our calculator analogy and see if we can develop a parallel. An early step in our average program called for us to enter a number. What does this step entail? Basically, as you can probably imagine, you key in a number one digit at a time and, when you're finished, you hit a button. That's input. You are providing the calculator with an element of data that it does not already have. After computing the average, you probably copy the answer onto a sheet of paper. That's output; you are transferring information from the calculator to some other medium. Input implies data going into the device; output implies answers or other results coming out from it.

Terminals (Fig. 1.2) are frequently used for getting data into and out from a computer. Imagine that you are a terminal operator. As the computer goes through its program (don't forget, it is working automatically, under control of a pre-supplied program) it eventually encounters an instruction that says, "Read input data." At this point, you, the terminal operator, would be asked to type a number or some other data (depending on the problem being solved) on your terminal and hit the RETURN key, thus sending the data into the computer. Later, when the computer encountered an instruction that told it to write output, the results would be printed on your terminal.

The terminal shown in Fig. 1.2 is a printing terminal; it resembles an electric typewriter. Another very popular type of terminal, resembling a television set with an attached keyboard, is shown in Fig. 1.3. Rather than printing input and output data, such CRT (for cathode ray tube) terminals display the characters on a screen.

Numerous other input and output devices could be cited. However, this book deals with the BASIC language, and BASIC, almost invariably, is a terminal language. Thus, we move on.

Storing the Program

Several times in the above discussion, we've mentioned that the computer acts under the control of a program. Where is this program found? How does the program get into the computer?

Let's deal with the first question first. The program is normally found in the computer's memory (Fig. 1.4). The control unit portion of the main processor, as you may recall, fetches an instruction from main memory and decodes it, passing control on to the arithmetic and logical unit, which executes the instruction. Then, it's back to the control unit, where another cycle begins. For this cycle to work, the program *must* be in main memory.

How does it get there? This question is not quite so easy. Imagine, to over simplify things a bit, that you have very carefully typed your program, and recorded a copy on a tape cassette. You load this cassette into the computer's tape reader, push a button on the computer's control console, and the program is copied into main memory.

Fig. 1.2: *A Terminal.*

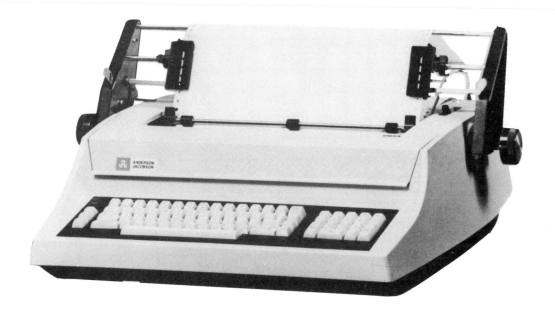

Fig. 1.3. *A CRT Terminal.*

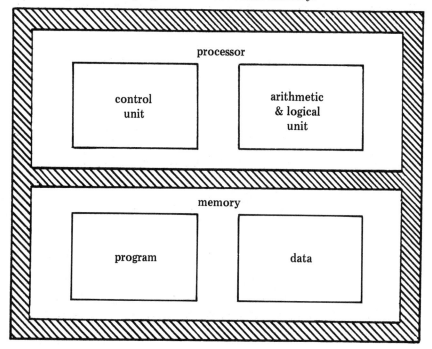

Some smaller computers work exactly this way. On larger computers, programs are stored on high-speed magnetic disk devices, and access is controlled by professional operators and special control programs, but the basic idea is the same. We'll consider this process in more detail later.

Storing the Data

What about the data? Where is it stored? Generally, what happens is that, on input, the data is also stored in main memory (Fig. 1.4). While in main memory, the data is processed; in other words, the data is moved around, and arithmetic is performed on it. When output is called for, the results are transferred from main memory to an output device.

The Computer: a Summary

In brief, that's what a computer is: a machine capable of performing a number of logical functions—arithmetic, copying, simple yes/no logic, input, and output. More importantly, it is possible for a human being to write a program consisting of a series of these logical functions and to introduce this program into the computer's main memory; once this has been done, the machine is capable of following the instructions of the program without further human intervention. In effect, given a program to provide control, a computer becomes an automatic machine. For any well defined, highly repetitive task, it's a very valuable machine, indeed.

We now know how to compute an average by hand. We also know a little bit about the computer. The next step is to develop a plan for implementing our solution on the computer.

Programmers use a number of different tools to aid in this detailed planning step; flowcharting is one of the more commonly used tools.

Flowcharting

A flowchart is a graphic representation of a program. Program logic (in other words, the arithmetic, the copy steps, the yes/no logic, and the input and output steps) is defined by using a few standard symbols (Fig. 1.5). These symbols are connected by lines to indicate the flow of logic through the program. Let's say, for example, that we want to read a card containing two numbers, to add the numbers, and to print the sum. A flowchart for this logic is illustrated in Fig. 1.6. Note that the flowchart very clearly defines two things. First, the symbols identify the individual logical steps in the program. Second, by following the lines connecting the symbols, the sequence of these steps is clearly defined. In other words, in addition to telling what must be done, a flowchart also defines the order in which these steps must be performed.

A few simple, generally accepted rules govern the flowlines. The normal direction of flow is from top to bottom or from left to right; arrowheads are used if the direction of flow is anything else. Flowlines should not cross. In general, the idea is to keep things as simple and as straightforward as is possible. To improve the readability of our flowcharts, we will follow the practice of always using arrowheads to indicate the direction of flow.

Look back at the manual solution we developed. Most of the instructions in that solution are pretty straightforward. "Enter a number" is obviously an input operation. "Push the ADD button" just as obviously calls for the execution of an addition operation. Almost without exception, the manual instructions have a direct match with the list of computer instructions presented earlier.

There is, however, one exception. Manual instruction 6 asks the question, "Are there any more numbers?". How do you know that there are no more numbers to be processed? Simple, says the human being, there are no more numbers to be processed. It's not that easy for a computer. The computer, don't forget, gets its data through an input device.

The human being operating the terminal would certainly recognize the fact that there are no more data *before* he or she tries to enter that data. The only way the computer can tell that there are no more data, however, is by asking the programmer or operator to enter some, only to be told that there are none. In other words, the computer cannot look ahead. It can react only to what has happened, and not to what is going to happen. This simple fact forces us to change our view of the problem solution.

Fig. 1.5: *Flowcharting Symbols.*

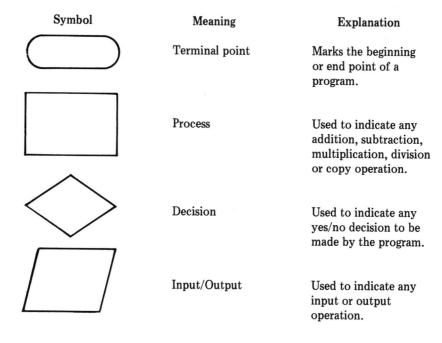

Symbol	Meaning	Explanation
	Terminal point	Marks the beginning or end point of a program.
	Process	Used to indicate any addition, subtraction, multiplication, division or copy operation.
	Decision	Used to indicate any yes/no decision to be made by the program.
	Input/Output	Used to indicate any input or output operation.

Fig. 1.6: *A simple flowchart.*

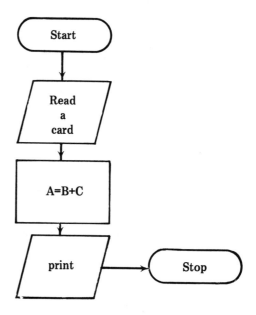

Let's flowchart how a computer would have to make the "no more data" decision (Fig. 1.7). Our flowchart begins with an input instruction. Following input, we ask a question: Is this the last of the data? There are two possible responses: yes or no. If the answer is "no," we process the data. If the answer is "yes," we perform end of data processing.

The fact that the end-of-data condition has been reached must be clearly and precisely communicated to the computer. How might the end-of-data test be implemented? Imagine, for example, that there are exactly 50 numbers to be averaged. The programmer might write instructions to count the number of data elements read; the end-of-data condition would then occur when this counter reached 50. Imagine instead that the task is to find the average of a number of examination grades ranging from a possible low of zero to a possible high of 100. After all the valid data have been entered, the operator might type an "impossible" value such as a negative number or a number exceeding 100 to indicate "end-of-data". Simple yes/no logic could then allow the program to test for this "impossible" condition.

In developing a solution to the "average" problem discussed in this chapter, we'll assume that we will be working with a set of positive numbers. After the last valid element of data has been read, we'll enter a negative number to indicate end-of-data. In Chapter 2, we'll see how a test for this condition can be implemented in BASIC.

Now we're ready to convert the human-level solution to the average problem into flowchart form. The finished flowchart might look like Figure 1.8. Let's go through it step by step; the steps have been numbered to aid in this process. Follow the flowchart carefully as we move through the program, and be sure that you understand exactly what happens in each and every step. The steps are:

1. This is the start of the program.

2. The accumulator is set to zero.

Fig. 1.7: *Testing for the "end-of-data" condition.*

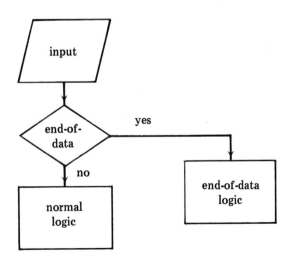

3. The counter is set to zero.

4. Read a value.

5. Test for end-of-data. Why do we want to test for end-of-data before accumulating and counting? Do we want to count the "impossible" negative value? Do we want to accumulate it? No.

6. If this is the end-of-data, skip to instruction 10, where we will compute the average.

7. If it's not, add the number to the accumulator.

8. Add 1 to the counter.

9. Go back and read another value (return to step 4).

10. Divide the accumulator by the counter to get the average. We reached this point, don't forget, only after the end-of-data condition had been encountered.

11. Send a line of output to the terminal.

12. End the program.

Our flowchart formally defines the logic of the soon-to-be-written program. We have used flowcharting as a planning aid, but it serves another important function as well. At some time in the future when we want to look back at our program and perhaps make some modifications, the flowchart serves as a reference document, clearly describing the logical flow of the program in an easy to follow form. Most programs, particularly business programs, will change over time. Thus, **documentation** is essential, and the flowchart is a very valuable documentation tool.

Defining the Data Fields

The flowchart defines the logical flow of the program, but if a computer is actually to execute this program, the programmer must define more than just the logic. Look back at Fig. 1.4, which shows both the program and the data being stored in main memory. We have a pretty good idea of what the program will contain, but what about the data?

Go through the flowchart (Fig. 1.8) once more, this time concentrating on the data. Block number 2 tells us to set the accumulator to zero; to do that, we must have an accumulator. The next block identifies a counter; we'll need a counter, too. Block number 4 tells us to read a value from the terminal. When that value comes into the computer, there must be space in main memory to hold it. Block number 7 refers to the value and the accumulator; we've already identified both. A similar argument can be advanced for adding a constant (1) to the counter; nothing new here, either. In block number 10, we discover that the average is computed by dividing the accumulator by the counter. Only the average is a new field. Thus, in writing this program, we are going to have to allow for the following data fields:

Fig. 1.8: *A flowchart of the Average Problem.*

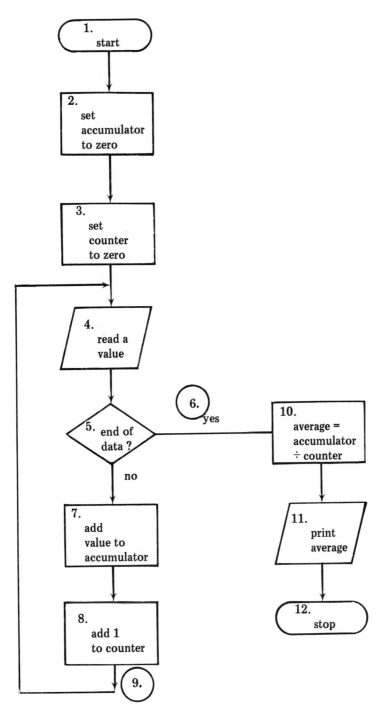

1. an accumulator,

2. a counter,

3. an input value,

4. the computed average.

Why bother defining the data fields before starting to write the code? For one thing, it helps you to avoid confusion. As you begin writing BASIC code, you will initially find the syntax of the language troublesome. As you concentrate on instruction number 60, it's easy to forget what was done in instruction 25. Defining the data fields first, means that you have one less thing to worry about as you write the program. Later, as your skill increases, you will be writing larger and more complex programs. Once again, it helps to work with pre-defined data fields.

Later, you will learn that more than one type of data can be manipulated on a computer. While we won't get into the details now, you will discover that distinguishing between character and numeric data is crucial, and defining the data fields first is by far the safest way to do it. In other languages, such as FORTRAN, COBOL, and PL/1, defining the precise content of the data fields is even more important than it is in BASIC.

CONVERTING OUR PLAN TO A COMPUTER PROGRAM

Finally, we are ready to begin writing the BASIC code. At this stage, we have defined the logical flow of the program (through a flowchart) and the data fields that are to be manipulated by the program. Once these factors have been defined, coding (as we'll see in Chapter 2) becomes little more than an exercise in translation.

SUMMARY

This chapter illustrated a reasonable approach for developing a computer-level solution to a problem. We began by carefully defining the problem to be solved. Next, we set up a straw person and planned a manual solution designed to tell this individual how to solve the problem. Throughout this discussion, we emphasized the value of desk checking.

After solving the problem at a human level, we were ready to move along to a computer-level solution. First, however, we found it necessary to describe a few basic computer concepts. A computer is capable of performing arithmetic, copying data from one memory location to another, performing simple yes/no logic, asking for input, and asking for output. The computer is a unique device in that it performs these functions automatically, under the direct control of a program stored in the computer's memory. A program is nothing more than a series of instructions, written by a programmer, designed to guide the computer through some logical function. A primary objective of this text is to teach you how to write such programs. Various input and output devices can be attached to a computer; we concentrated on terminals.

Moving from a manual solution to a computer program, we went through a number of detailed planning steps. First, using flowcharting as a planning aid, we carefully defined the logic of the program. Of particular interest was the way a computer recognizes the fact that the last of the data has been read. Once the logic was defined, we moved along to the data, defining all the data fields to be manipulated by the program. Having laid the ground work, we are now ready to code the program in BASIC, the topic of Chapter 2.

EXERCISES

1. An instructor would like to apply a grade curve to an exam so that the class average comes out to exactly 78. This means that if the actual class average is greater than 78, points will be deducted from every student's score and, if the actual average is less than 78, points will be added to every student's score. The easiest way to do this is to find the actual average and then to compute the difference between this figure and the target of 78. How would you modify the problem solution developed in this chapter to implement the extra computation? Add the new computation to the flowchart. The output will now consist of the computed average and the difference between this average and 78.

2. A baseball player's batting average is computed by dividing the number of times at bat into the number of hits. Since hits cannot possibly exceed times at bat, this statistic will always be a fraction (exception: 1.000); usually it's computed correct to three decimal places. Plan a computer-level solution, including a flowchart, to produce a list of the player number, times at bat, hits, and computed batting average of each of the 25 players on a team.

3. An instructor has indicated that each student's final grade will be computed according to the following formula:

$$\text{exam no. 1} \ldots\ldots\ldots 25\%$$

$$\text{exam no. 2} \ldots\ldots\ldots 25\%$$

$$\text{homework} \ldots\ldots\ldots 20\%$$

$$\text{final exam} \ldots\ldots\ldots 30\%$$

Assume that your actual grades for each of these four grade factors will be typed into a terminal (actual grades are on a scale of 0 - 100). Plan a computer-level solution to read the four grades, compute the percentage value of each of the factors, sum the factor values, and print this final "total grade points" value.

4. A common computer application involves printing address labels for mailings. Assume that you have a series of names and addresses written on a deck of 3 x 5 cards, one name and address per card. Assume that the straw person of this chapter is your secretary, and prepare a set of instructions telling this individual how to prepare

properly addressed envelopes from these cards. Once you have completed the human-level instructions, expand your planning to a computer-level solution.

5. Every student knows how his or her school computes a grade point average. Plan a computer-level solution to the problem of computing your own. Your solution should be general; in other words, do *not* assume that the list of courses and associated credit hours and grades are known before the computation begins. If your school uses letter grades, you may convert to a numerical equivalent on input, replacing A's with 4's, B's with 3's, and so on.

6. Imagine that a student is to be paid 1 cent today, 2 cents tomorrow, 4 cents the day after, and so on, with each day's pay exactly doubling that of the day before. How would you go about computing the total amount (cumulative) earned by the student after 30 days? Develop a flowchart.

7. Develop a flowchart for a program to make change. The program should accept the amount paid and the amount of purchase; the total change due is the difference between these two numbers. The logic should, given this amount of change, determine the proper number of dollars, quarters, dimes, nickels, and pennies due the customer.

8. There are four scales to measure temperature: Fahrenheit, Centegrade, Kelvin, and Rankine. We want to generate a conversion table. For Fahrenheit temperatures ranging from 0° to 222° in intervals of 10°, list the equivalent temperature in the other three scales. You will, of course, need conversion factors; you should be able to find them in any chemistry book or in an encyclopedia. Develop a flowchart.

9. Develop a flowchart for a program to compute and print the sum of the first 200 integers.

10. As we enter the 1980s, the population of the United States is estimated to be 226 million, while Mexico's population is estimated at 66 million. Assume that our population growth rate is 0.9%, while Mexico's is 2.8%. In what year will Mexico pass the United States in population if these trends continue? Develop the algorithms and a flowchart to solve this problem.

2

Writing the Program in BASIC

In Chapter 1, we developed a solution to a problem. In this chapter we will write the "average" program in the BASIC language, and then show you how to execute the program on a computer.

THE FUNCTION OF A PROGRAM

The basic difference between a computer and a calculator is that a calculator requires human intervention at each step in a process, while a computer works automatically, under the control of a program stored in its main memory. The program consists of a series of instructions. Each instruction tells the computer to do one thing: add, subtract, compare, and so on.

A computer's basic function is processing data. Consider, for example, the average program we are about to write. The data consists of a series of numbers. The program will consist of a series of instructions designed to accumulate and count these numbers, to compute their average, and to print the result. Specific instructions, executed in a specific sequence will lead to the desired result. The starting point is the data, the numbers. The objective is the computed average. The program's function is to control the computer as it processes the data into the desired output information.

Of course, the instructions must be written in a form that the computer can understand. Inside the machine, everything—programs and data—is stored in binary form. At one time, programmers actually had to code in pure binary, machine language form, but the modern programmer writes in any of a number of more human-like languages that can be translated to binary by the computer itself. BASIC, the Beginners All-purpose Symbolic Instruction Code, is such a language. Its statements resemble algebraic expressions.

BASIC DATA

The key function of a program is to process data. The data is first stored in main memory. The program's instructions manipulate that data; the results are then available for output.

A computer's main memory is divided into a number of independently accessible memory locations. Each element of data occupies one or more such locations. In our average program, for example, we will set aside space to hold the input value, the counter, the accumulator, and the computed average. How do we indicate our need for space to hold these elements of data? How do we differentiate between the space set aside to hold the counter, and the space set aside to hold the accumulator?

In the BASIC language, we solve both problems by defining a **variable name** for each element of data used by the program. The rules for defining variable names are very simple:

> A BASIC variable name consists of a single letter or a
>
> single letter followed by a single digit.

Valid variable names would thus include: A, A0, A1, B8, and so on. In writing the average program we might define the following four variable names:

A	the accumulator
C	the counter
X	the input value
M	the computed average (or mean).

The choice of variable names is up to the programmer. It makes sense, however, to use names that imply something about the use of the element of data; in defining the accumulator, "A" is better than "Z" simply because "A" is the first letter in the word accumulator. Note that it really doesn't matter to the computer; an intelligent choice of variable names is strictly for the convenience of the programmer.

THE INPUT STATEMENT

Typically, the data to be processed exists as numbers on a sheet of paper, or holes punched in a deck of cards, or values recorded on some other medium. Before this data can be processed it must be transferred into the computer. In BASIC, input operations are controlled by an **INPUT** statement. The basic form of the INPUT statement is:

```
statement no.    INPUT    var1, var2, var3, . . .
```

Every BASIC statement must be preceeded by a **statement number**; more about these numbers later. Following the statement number is the word INPUT, followed, in turn, by a list of variable names separated by commas.

In our average program, for example, a value is to be read from the input device and stored in a memory location called X. The instruction:

    30 INPUT X

would tell the computer to input a single value and store it in a memory location named X.

Imagine that, in another program, we want to compute the area of a rectangle. We need the width and the length of the rectangle to find its area. The instruction:

    50 INPUT W,L

tells the computer to read two numbers from the input device, store the first one in a memory location named W, and store the second value in a memory location named

L. Later, by referring to these variable names, we'll be able to retrieve the two values and use them in computations.

THE LET STATEMENT

The **LET statement** is the BASIC data manipulation statement; it allows the programmer to copy data and to perform arithmetic. Let's consider the simple copy function first. The first two steps in the average program involve setting the accumulator and the counter to zero (look back at the flowchart). How can we do this? The answer is really quite simple. Consider the following two statements:

        10 LET A = 0

        20 LET C = 0

What do they do? The first statement, number 10, says to copy whatever is on the right side of the equal sign into the memory location specified on the left side of the equal sign; in other words, copy the constant 0 into the memory location named A. The second statement says much the same thing, copying a 0 into the memory location to which the name C has been assigned.

What is a **constant**? A constant is an element of data whose value never changes. Numeric constants in BASIC are written by simply writing the numeric value; for example, 0, 1, 1.5, 3.1416, 2.71828, and 1324.35 are all valid numeric constants. They can be written with or without a decimal point, as appropriate. For very large or very small numbers, a form of scientific notation can be used. The speed of light, roughly 186,000 miles per second, can, for example, be expressed as 0.186×10^6 in scientific notation. A BASIC equivalent would be 0.186E6, where the letter E indicates the basic 10 raised to a power.

The general form of a LET statement is:

```
statement no.   LET   variable = expression
```

You must have a valid variable name on the left side of the equal sign. We've already seen that a simple constant is one example of the expression that follows the equal sign. The BASIC programmer is not, however, limited to coding constants. The **expression** can also be used to specify arithmetic operations.

There are five arithmetic **operators** that are recognized by BASIC:

        +   for addition

        −   for subtraction

| * | for multiplication |

| / | for division |

| ↑ or ** | for exponentiation (raising to a power). |

The programmer codes the rough equivalent of algebraic statements by using these operators in combination with variables and constants. For example, the area of a rectangle is the product of the length and the width. A BASIC expression to compute this area might be:

    L * W

A LET statement using this expression might be:

    100 LET A = L * W

This instruction tells the computer to take the values currently stored in the memory locations named L and W, multiply them, and place the product in the memory location A.

The formula for computing the area of a circle is

$$\text{area} = \pi \, (\text{radius})^2$$

An equivalent BASIC LET statement might be:

    80 LET A = 3.1416 * R ↑ 2

or

    80 LET A = 3.1416 * R ** 2

The Sequence of Operations

In what order are arithmetic operations performed? It does make a difference. Consider, for example, the following simple expression:

    5 * 2 + 2.

If the expression is evaluated from left to right, the multiplication is done first (5 * 2 = 10), and then the addition is done (10 + 2 = 12); the answer is 12. If, on the other hand, the expression is evaluated from right to left, the addition will be done first (2 + 2 = 4), followed by the multiplication (10 * 2 = 20), yielding an answer of 20. Obviously both cannot be correct. The order does make a difference.

The rules for determining the order in which the operations in a BASIC expression will be performed are the same rules you learned in algebra:

1. raising a value to a power (exponentiation) is first,

2. multiplication and division are second,

3. addition and subtraction are last.

What if there are two additions or a multiplication and a division in a single expression? When such "ties" occur, the operations are performed from left to right.

These rules are not always adequate. Consider, for example, a problem in which the sum of two variables, A + B, is to be multiplied by the constant 2. The expression:

A + B * 2

would yield the wrong answer because, given the rules of BASIC, the multiplication (B * 2) would be done first. We can get around the problem by using parentheses; for example:

(A + B) * 2

Just as in algebra, anything that is enclosed within a set of parentheses must be done first.

Now, consider a more complex expression, such as:

((A + B) * C) ↑ 2

A set of parentheses surrounds the terms ((A + B) * C), but inside this set of parentheses is another set! What comes first? The rules does not change: do what is within the parentheses. Thus, the first step is to add A and B, which completes the operation specified within the inner parentheses. Now, multiplication can be performed. Finally, when all functions within the parentheses are complete, the result can be raised to the second power.

Most versions of BASIC allow the programmer to nest as many as three sets of parentheses; many allow more. If, however, an expression becomes so complex that it requires several levels of parentheses, that expression can become very difficult to understand. Thus, it is often better to write a complex function as a series of BASIC LET statements, each one computing part of the answer. A series of simple instructions is almost always better than a single complex instruction.

THE SEQUENCE OF INSTRUCTIONS

It is one thing to write a valid INPUT statement or a LET statement. It is quite a different thing to determine what statement should be written "next." A BASIC program consists of a series of BASIC statements, and both the individual statements and their order must be correct if the program is to produce the desired output.

One of the first rules you must learn as you begin to write programs is that the computer assumes nothing. Consider, for example, the simple LET statement:

```
50  LET  X = Y + Z
```

What is the value of X? Unless you know the values of Y and Z, you have no way of answering this question. Neither does the computer. In other words, that statement, all by itself, is meaningless.

Consider instead the following series of instructions:

```
30  LET  Y = 10

40  LET  Z = 20

50  LET  X = Y + Z
```

Now, what is the value of X? The answer, clearly, is 30. As an alternative, we might code the following sequence of instructions:

```
40  INPUT  Y,Z

50  LET  X = Y + Z
```

Now the values of Y and Z will be entered by the programmer when the INPUT statement is executed, and X will be the sum of whatever values are input.

The point is very simple. The value of every term on the right side of the equal sign must be known *before* the LET statement is coded. In the statement:

```
30  LET  Y = 10
```

the number 10 is a constant, and the value of a constant is always known. The statement:

```
50  LET  X = Y + Z
```

is valid only if previous statements have assigned values to both Y and Z. Failure to follow this simple rule is a common source of error among beginners.

CONTROL STATEMENTS

Every BASIC statement must have a statement number. This number serves two primary purposes. First, the statement numbers determine the sequence in which the statements will be executed; the lowest numbered statement comes first and the highest numbered statement, last. We suggest that you leave gaps between the numbers of consecutive statements, using 10, 20, 30, . . . rather than 1, 2, 3, . . ., and so on. As you begin writing programs, you will occasionally forget a statement. If you want to insert a statement between numbers 20 and 30, you can call it statement number 25. Although you may be typing it after statement number 100 has been entered, BASIC will take care of inserting it where it belongs.

The second function of the statement number is to uniquely identify the statement. Consider, for example, our average program. We want to read a value, count it, accumulate it, and then read another value, repeating this cycle until there is no more data. Since we want to execute the same statements over and over again, we need a statement to return control to the INPUT statement. Our *loop* might be coded as:

70 INPUT X

80 LET A = A + X

90 LET C = C + 1

100 GOTO 70

The **GOTO** statement transfers control to the specified statement number, in this case, 70. The general form of the GOTO statement is

```
statement no.    GOTO    statement no.
```

In the example above, the program would input a value for X, accumulate it, count it, and then go back to statement number 70 to input another value of X.

There is only one thing wrong with the logic coded above; there is no way out of that loop. Those four statements will be endlessly executed over and over again. When do we want to terminate the loop? When we run out of data. How can we identify that condition? Since, in this problem, we are assuming that the numbers to be averaged are all positive, the programmer can simply enter a negative number to signify the end of data. Now all we need is a mechanism that allows the program to recognize a negative number.

That mechanism is the **IF** statement. Its general form is:

```
statement no.   IF   expr-1   condition   expr-2   THEN   statement no.
```

where expr-1 and expr-2 are BASIC expressions. In testing for a negative value of X, for example, we might code:

80 IF X < 0 THEN 120.

If the condition (X is less than 0) is true, we branch (or GOTO) statement number 120. If it is false, we don't branch.

Any valid BASIC expression can be used, although most programmers tend to use simple variables and constants for clarity. Valid conditions include:

=	equal to
<	less than
>	greater than
>=	greater than or equal to
<=	less than or equal to
<>	not equal to

Adding an IF test for a negative value to our program loop produces the following code:

```
 70  INPUT  X
 80  IF  X  <  0  THEN  120
 90  LET  A = A + X
100  LET  C = C + 1
110  GOTO  70
```

We have yet to code statement number 120, but it obviously follows statement 110.

The IF statement implements simple yes/no logic. A test is set up, comparing the value of the first expression to the second. The condition is either true (X *is* less than 0), or it is false; there is no other possibility. If the condition is true, control is given to the indicated instruction—the one whose number follows the word THEN. If the condition is false, control passes to the next instruction in sequence, as if the IF statement weren't even there.

OUTPUT

A computer would be useless if human beings could not see the results of its computations; output is essential. The primary output statement in BASIC is the PRINT statement. The general form of a PRINT statement is:

```
statement no.    PRINT    var-1,  literal-1,  var-2,  . . .
```

where var-1 is a variable, and literal-1 is a literal. Any number of variables and literals can be printed in any order. Consider, for example, the output from the average program. We want to print the computed average; the variable we are using to hold this value is M. It might be a good idea to print a message telling us what the number represents. A good PRINT statement for this problem might be

130 PRINT "AVERAGE = "; M

The letter M is a variable name. The "AVERAGE = " is a literal constant. When the computer prints or displays a literal constant, it prints "literally" whatever is enclosed in the set of quotation marks. When a variable is printed, the computer prints or displays the current value of that variable.

It is possible to include a number of different variable names in a single print statement; simply separate the names by commas. Literal constants can be interspersed as desired; once again, separate any two variable names, any two literals, or any combination of a literal and a variable name by a comma.

In the example cited above we used a semicolon (;) rather than a comma to separate the literal and the variable name. Why? BASIC normally breaks the output line into a series of zones of perhaps 20 characters each, and prints one item (a variable or a literal) in each zone. Sometimes, this standard results in output that is difficult to read, with related fields widely separated; for example:

AVERAGE =   20.5

By using a semicolon instead of a comma, this standard is ignored. Instead, a few spaces (usually two) are left between the adjacent fields. The output resulting from:

130 PRINT "AVERAGE = "; M

would be

AVERAGE =   20.5

which is much easier to read.

ENDING THE PROGRAM

The last statement in every BASIC program must be an END statement; the general form is:

> statement no.   END

The purpose of the END statement is twofold. First, when the BASIC program is being translated into machine level instructions, the END statement indicates that there are no more instructions to be translated. Later, when the program is executing, the END statement tells the computer system that the program is finished.

WRITING THE AVERAGE PROGRAM IN BASIC

We have now covered all the BASIC statements we will need to write the average program. One more statement is, however, worthy of mention, the **REM statement**. The REM statement is used to provide remarks for documentation; these remarks are used to explain what the other statements do. Remarks or comments are always optional, but you will probably find at least a minimal level of documentation essential. Our practice in this text will be to begin each program with a block of REM statements identifying the programmer and the function of the program.

Let's turn our attention to the average program. We will be using the following variable names:

A	the accumulator
C	the counter
X	the input value
M	the computed average (mean).

We also have, from Chapter 1, a flowchart (reproduced as Fig. 2.1). Our objective is to convert this flowchart into BASIC code.

We'll start with a set of comments, using REM statements:

```
10              REM * PROGRAM TO COMPUTE AN AVERAGE.

20              REM *    WRITTEN BY: W.S. DAVIS

30              REM *              1/10/81

40              REM * * * * * * * * * * * * * * * * * *
```

The remarks identify the program and the programmer. Why did we skip so many spaces between the statement number and REM? The remarks are not really part of the program. They are for documentation, for support. If we shift the comments over to the right, and leave the regular BASIC statements aligned near the statement numbers on the left, we'll have an obvious visual separation between the primary instructions and the support instructions; in other words, the REMs will be able to do their job without getting in the way. (Note, however, that not all versions of BASIC allow you to insert such blanks.)

Next we'll go through the flowchart step by step, writing a BASIC statement to implement the logic of each step. First, we must set the accumulator and the counter to zero. We can do this by coding:

Fig. 2.1: *A flowchart of the Average Problem.*

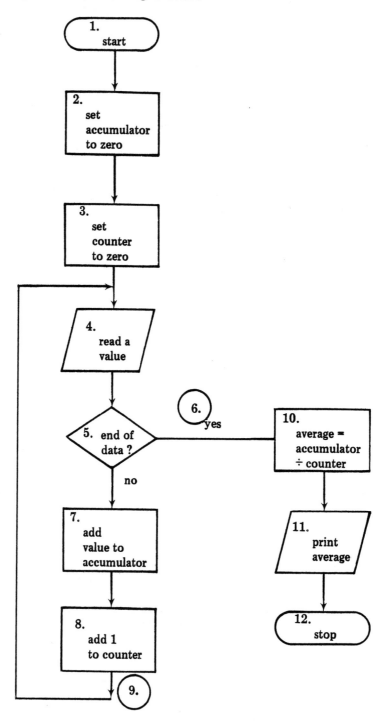

```
50 LET  A = 0

60 LET  C = 0
```

Following the initialization of these two work fields, we enter the loop that reads, counts, and accumulates values. It was coded in an earlier example:

```
 70  INPUT  X

 80  IF  X < 0  THEN  120

 90  LET  A = A + X

100  LET  C = C + 1

110  GOTO  70
```

We are now ready to code the last instructions in the program:

```
120  LET  M = A / C

130  PRINT  "AVERAGE = "; M

140  END
```

The completed program might look like Fig. 2.2.

Fig. 2.2: *The average program in BASIC.*


```
 10                       REM * PROGRAM TO COMPUTE AN AVERAGE
 20                       REM *    WRITTEN BY: W.S. DAVIS
 30                       REM *            1/10/81
 40                       REM * * * * * * * * * * * * * * * *
 50 LET A=0
 60 LET C=0
 70 INPUT X
 80 IF X<0 THEN 120
 90 LET A=A+X
100 LET C=C+1
110 GOTO 70
120 LET M=A/C
130 PRINT "AVERAGE = ";M
140 END
```

RUNNING THE PROGRAM

Finally, after all this preparation, we are ready to run the program on the computer. This is the acid test. If we have been precise and accurate in writing the program, it will work. If not, it won't. A program that is 85% right is simply not good enough. If the logic is not perfect, the program will not work.

The specific details associated with entering and running a program will vary significantly from system to system; ask your instructor how your system works. Although the details do differ, general ideas do not. Let's consider how a student might enter and run this program on a typical computer system. We'll refer to the terminal listing of Fig. 2.3, which was prepared under control of a Hewlett-Packard 3000 series II computer, Note that everything typed by the programmer is shown in lower case, and everything printed by the computer appears in upper case (capital) letters.

Signing On

The first hurdle the beginning programmer must cross is signing on the computer system. Computer time is valuable and expensive. Most systems are designed to make certain that only authorized persons use the computer. Before you can begin working, you must prove you are an authorized person, usually by giving the computer a valid user number, password, or both before being allowed to proceed.

Specific procedures for signing on vary significantly from installation to installation. Typically, a student is required first to depress the RETURN key on the terminal keyboard. A message normally follows, asking for a user number (see Fig. 2.3, near the top). Frequently, the next message asks for a second identification code, a password. Often, neither the user number nor the password is printed or displayed; this is to make it difficult for anyone to "steal" the computer access codes. On some systems, only a user number is needed; on others, only a password. Your instructor will explain exactly how to sign onto your system.

Once you are signed on, the next step is to tell the system that you plan to write programs in BASIC. With the exception of a small, personal microcomputer, most systems are capable of translating statements written in a number of different languages. To avoid confusion, it is only reasonable that you specify the one you will be using. Once again, the specific procedure for identifying BASIC varies from system to system; typically, the student types ENTER BASIC or simply BASIC (Fig. 2.3) and then hits the RETURN key. Once again, ask your instructor how your system works.

You are now "on" the system. The next step is to begin writing the BASIC instructions.

Typing the Program

Entering your BASIC program is quite simple: Type a statement number followed by the BASIC statement, and then hit the RETURN key. When the system is ready for the next statement, it will type or display a "prompt" symbol; often a question mark, a

Entering and running the average program on a typical system
(a Hewlett-Packard 3000 series II)

```
:hello student.miami
HP3000 / MPE III B.01.0B.  TUE, FEB  5, 1980,  1:40 PM
WELCOME TO THE HP/3000 MINICOMPUTER. HAVE A NICE DAY.
:basic

HP32101B.00.11(4WD)  BASIC  (C)HEWLETT-PACKARD CO 1979
>10                      rem * program to compute an average.
>20                      rem *   written by: w.s. davis
>30                      rem *            1/10/81
>40                      rem * * * * * * * * * * * * * *
>50 ler a = 0
ERROR@2
>50 let a = 0
>60 let c = 0
>70 input x
>80 if x < 0 then 120
>90 let a = a + x
>100 let c = c + 1
>110 goto 70
>120 let m = a/c
>130 print "AVERAGE = ";m
>140 end
>list
   10 REM                    REM * PROGRAM TO COMPUTE AN AVERAGE
   20 REM                    REM *   WRITTEN BY: W.S. DAVIS
   30 REM                    REM *            1/10/81
   40 REM                    REM * * * * * * * * * * * * * * * *
   50 LET A=0
   60 LET C=0
   70 INPUT X
   80 IF X<0 THEN 120
   90 LET A=A+X
  100 LET C=C+1
  110 GOTO 70
  120 LET M=A/C
  130 PRINT "AVERAGE = ";M
  140 END
>run
?10
?15
?20
?-1
AVERAGE =  15

>exit

END OF SUBSYSTEM
:bye
```

colon, or a "greater than" symbol (Fig. 2.3), depending on the system. Repeat the process, typing a statement number, the statement, and then hit the RETURN key.

What if you make a mistake, and type:

50 LER A = 0

for example? On some systems, you will get an error message immediately following the incorrect statement (see Fig. 2.3 again). On others, the error message will be generated after all the statements have been entered and the program is executed. Perhaps you recognized the error as soon as you hit the RETURN button. The solution to the problem is identical in any case: simply retype the statement using the same statement number:

50 LET A = 0

The new version of statement 50 (or whatever number you used) will replace the old version.

Many systems have elaborate procedures for correcting errors, which allow the programmer to change single characters or strings of characters without affecting the entire instruction. Such procedures vary significantly from system to system. As you become more experienced in programming, you will probably want to learn some of these techniques. For the beginner, however, they can often be confusing, hindering rather than helping the task of writing a program. Simply retype the incorrect line. This procedure will work on virtually any version of BASIC. What could be easier?

Running the Program

After all the BASIC statements have been typed into the computer, you are ready to run the program. On most systems, a simple command such as LIST (Fig. 2.3) will produce a current list of the program statements for your visual verification; it's a good idea to get such a list. If anything is wrong, correct it now; once again, any incorrect statements can simply be retyped.

Assuming that everything is in order, it's time to start the program. Although some systems are different, normally the programmer is required to type only the single word, RUN. Your first contact with the program will probably be a prompt character, a question mark, for example (Fig. 2.3, near the bottom). The program is asking for input data. In response to a question mark, the programmer types a number and hits RETURN. Another question mark appears, and another value is input. This happens over and over again, until all the data has been entered. Following the entry of the last value, the system will print or display yet another question mark; it, after all, does not yet know that there is no more data. The program was designed to recognize a negative number as an end-of-data indicator; thus, enter any negative number. The computed average is then printed, and the program ends.

Is the answer correct? We entered a very simple set of data, the numbers 10, 15, and 20. We know what the average should be: 15. The answer generated by our program is correct; thus the program is probably correct. This little trick, typing in a set of test data for which the answer is known, is a way to check the program. Now, with real confidence in our program, we can enter our data and use the computer to compute an average of a set of numbers whose mean we don't know.

Signing Off

Our first computer program is finished; it's time to sign-off. On the Hewlett-Packard system, we type EXIT, wait for a prompt, and type BYE. On other systems, the student must type SIGNOFF, OFF, or some other command. Check with your instructor for the valid sign-off procedures on your system.

THE PROGRAM DEVELOPMENT PROCESS

Writing a program consists of at least two clearly identifiable steps. The first is *logical*: What instruction should I write next? This logical function calls for careful planning, and careful thought. Chapter 1 was devoted to this logical function. The second step is largely *mechanical*: How should I write this specific instruction? Chapter 2 was concerned with the mechanics of writing the BASIC instructions needed to implement the already planned average program.

Anyone can learn the mechanics of coding; all it takes is practice. The rules and syntax of BASIC may seem confusing right now, but if you stick with it, writing the code will become easy. It is just a matter of time and effort.

The real problem is logic. Planning the proper sequence of steps in a program requires careful thought, careful planning, and a moderate degree of aptitude. It is this ability to think, to logically define the solution to a problem as a series of program instructions, that earns a person the title "programmer".

All too often, the beginner tends to lose sight of this essential fact. For obvious reasons, programming texts start with examples involving relatively simple logic—the computation of an average, for example. The logic seems obvious; the task of coding that logic seems relatively difficult, simply because the beginner has never written code before. The result is predictable. The student becomes so concerned with the mechanics that he or she, figuratively, "cannot see the forest for the trees". The *real* problem is defining the correct logic. The *perceived* problem becomes one of writing instructions in BASIC (or some other language).

Is this unusual? Not at all. Have you ever known a student whose excessive concern for spelling and punctuation, the mechanics of writing, interfered with the ability to write a decent paper? Have you ever known a student who failed to grasp the underlying concept being presented in an analytical course because of excessive concern with the mechanics of manipulating algebraic symbols? Perhaps you have missed a key idea in a history course because of an excessive concern with names, dates, and places.

How can you avoid this problem as you begin to learn how to program? The answer is really quite simple: *Do your planning first*. Force yourself to:

1. define all key variables or data fields, and

2. define the logical flow of the program using either psuedocode, flowcharts, or both,

before writing a single line of code. If you take the time to do this, the task of coding will be reduced simply to translating already defined operations, one at a time, into the BASIC language. The key question: "What instruction should I code next?", will have been answered. In effect, you will have already mapped the forest; then, you can worry about the trees.

Try it. It works.

SUMMARY

In this chapter, using the BASIC language, we wrote the average program planned in Chapter 1. First, the rules for defining a variable name in BASIC were defined: a variable name consists of a single letter or a single letter followed by a single digit. Next, the INPUT statement was described; it allows the programmer to transfer data into a program. The LET statement is the BASIC data manipulation statement, allowing arithmetic operations to be defined. The sequence of operations is the same as that found in algebra. By using GOTO and IF statements, the programmer can control the sequence in which instructions are executed. Output is achieved by coding a PRINT statement. The last statement in each program must be an END statement.

Having defined the BASIC statements, we coded the program, translating the flowchart developed in Chapter 1 into a BASIC instructions. We then illustrated how this program would be run on a typical computer system. The chapter ended with a brief discussion of the program development process; this section stressed the value of planning a solution *before* beginning to write code.

Note

Additional BASIC syntax details can be found in Module A, immediately following this chapter. You may want to read this material before completing the exercises below.

EXERCISES

1. The formula for finding the area of a circle is:

$$\text{AREA} = \pi r^2$$

where π = 3.1416, and "r" is the radius. Write a program to compute and print the area of a circle of radius 5.25.

2.   Modify program 1 so that it computes the area of a circle of any radius. Use an INPUT statement to provide the value of the radius. Repeat the program for several values, using an IF statement to test for the end of data condition; devise a reasonable test for end of data.

3.   The volume of a cylinder can be computed by the formula:

$$v = \pi r^2 h,$$

where π = 3.1416,

r = radius,

h = height.

Write a program to input the value of radius and height and compute the volume. Print the answer.

4.   A baseball player's batting average can be computed by dividing hits by times at bat. Write a program to input, for each player, hits and times at bat, compute the batting average, and then print the player's times at bat, hits, and computed batting average. Note that there might be as few as nine and as many as twenty-five players on the team. Devise a reasonable end of data check.

5.   The Pythagorean Theorem says that, given the length of any two sides (a and b) of a right triangle, the formula:

$$c = \sqrt{a^2 + b^2}$$

can be used to find the length of the third side. Write a program to compute and print the length of the third side given the input of the lengths of the other two sides. Note: the square root of X is X ↑ 0.5.

6.   The outer radius of a flat washer is eight inches. The inner radius (the radius of the hole) is six inches. Compute and print the area of the washer.

7.   If light travels 186,000 miles per second, how far does it travel in 3.5 years?

8.   The area of a triangle can be found by using the formula:

$$area = \sqrt{S\ (S\text{-}a)\ (S\text{-}b)\ (S\text{-}c)}$$

where a, b, and c are the lengths of the three sides, and:

$$S = \frac{a + b + c}{2}$$

Write a program to compute and print the area of a triangle using this formula.

9.   In 1626 the Indians sold Manhattan Island to the Dutch for roughly $24. If they had invested this money at 8% interest, what would it be worth today? The

formula for computing interest earned is:

$$W = P (1 + i)^n$$

where:
W = future value (in this case, the value today),

P = the original investment (in this case, $24).

i = the interest rate,

n = the number of years.

10. Write the program planned in exercise 1, Chapter 1.

11. Write Chapter 1, exercise 3.

12. Write Chapter 1, exercise 5.

13. A baseball pitcher's earned run average is computed by using the following formula:

$$ERA = (earned\ runs) / (equivalent\ nine\ inning\ games),$$

where the term (equivalent nine inning games) is computed by dividing the actual innings pitched by nine. Write a program to compute and print the earned run averages for a number of players.

14. A quadratic equation of the form

$$Ax^2 + Bx + C = 0$$

has a pair of solutions which can be computed by solving:

$$x = \frac{-B \pm \sqrt{B^2 - 4AC}}{2A}$$

Write a program to input values for A, B, and C, and compute the two roots. Remember that you cannot take the square root of a negative number. Consider using several simple expressions instead of one complex expression.

Module

BASIC
Syntax

Chapter 1 was concerned with planning a solution to a problem; in Chapter 2, we implemented that solution in the BASIC language. The emphasis of these two chapters was on the entire program development process. Coding, the task of actually writing the instructions, is but one step in this process. You can *learn to write code.* **Anyone** *can learn to write code; all it takes is practice. The real trick to programming is knowing what instruction to write next. If a problem solution has been carefully planned* **before** *coding begins, the programmer will* **know** *what instruction to code next, and the task of writing the instructions will become a largely mechanical process.*

The fact that coding is (or should be) largely mechanical does not, however, mean that it is a trivial problem. The purpose of a program is to tell a computer (a machine) how to perform some function. The instructions that make up the program must be **precise,** *or the computer will be unable to understand them. Coding requires extreme attention to detail. The programmer must follow the syntax rules of the language.*

If you are a typical beginner, you will find the rules and syntax of the BASIC language a bit confusing at first. This feeling passes, usually with the successful completion of your first program or two. All it takes is practice. That is the purpose of this module: to provide you with some practice in BASIC syntax. A number of drill exercises are included; the answers to these drill exercises can be found in the Appendix in the back of the book.

ARITHMETIC EXPRESSIONS

Constants

A constant is a value that does not change throughout the execution of a program. In BASIC, numeric constants are coded by simply writing the number; for example, 12, 2.5, and 3.1416. There are, however, a few rules that limit the numbers you can write. For example:

1. *Positive numbers.* A plus sign (+) may be coded but is normally not needed.

2. *Negative numbers.* A negative sign (−) must be coded.

3. *Commas* may not be coded within the number. For example, 186,000 is illegal; 186000 would be correct.

4. *Spaces* may not be left within a constant. For example, 123   456 is illegal under most versions of BASIC.

5. *The decimal point* is optional when coding whole numbers; 5, 5., and 5.0 all mean the same thing.

   [Note, however, that on **some** *versions of BASIC there is a difference between 5 and 5.0. The former number, without the decimal point, is called an* **integer***; with the decimal point, it becomes a* **real** *number. This distinction is not a standard feature of the language.]*

Very large and very small numbers can be represented in scientific notation. For example, the speed of light is roughly 186,000 miles per second. Using scientific notation, this value can be written as 0.186×10^6. The power of ten (in this case, the 6) indicates how many places the decimal point must be moved to the right. Very small numbers can be represented by using a negative power of ten. For example, an angstrom unit is defined as one-hundred millionth of a centemeter, or 0.00000001 centemeter. In scientific notation this value becomes 0.1×10^{-7}. Both the speed of light and the angstrom unit are shown in what is called *normalized* form, with the first significant digit immediately following the decimal point. As an alternative, we could have written 1.86×10^5 and 1.0×10^{-8}; show why these two forms are equivalent to the values shown above.

BASIC numeric constants can be coded using a form of scientific notation. The "x10" is present in any number written in scientific form. To code BASIC constants, the programmer replaces the "x10" with the letter E. The speed of light can be written as 1.86E5, while the length of an angstrom unit becomes 1.0E−8. Preceeding the letter E is the numeric portion of the constant; following the E is the power of ten. Such numbers are called *real* numbers or *floating-point* numbers.

There are limits on the size of a BASIC constant. These limits are imposed by the internal circuitry of a given computer, and thus it is not surprising to discover that the limits vary from system to system. Under *minimal* BASIC, the programmer is restricted to no more than six digits of precision, and the biggest power of ten allowed is 38.

Thus, numbers as big as 0.999999E38 or as small as 0.999999E−38 can be stored by a BASIC program. If the exponent is bigger than 38, an overflow condition occurs, and the program will probably fail. If the exponent is smaller than −38, an underflow condition occurs. If more than six digits are coded, the low-order digits are usually ignored. Incidently, the six-digit limit holds on regular (non-scientific) numbers too.

Some computers allow for as many as 15 digits of precision. Numbers as big as 10^{74} and as small as 10^{-74} are not uncommon. Check the system reference manual for the limits on your machine.

EXERCISES:

1. Which of the following constants are correct? Which are incorrect, and why?

   a. 12   d. 123,456   g. +398   j. 1.25E+7

   b. 12.0   e. 123456.78   h. −927   k. 1.7732E−24

   c. 25.25 1   f. +123456   i. 0.5E50   l. 123456E32

2. You should be able to find the values for many of the following in a good dictionary. Write each as a BASIC constant.

   a. Pi (or π).

   b. A conversion factor for centemeters to inches.

   c. A conversion factor for meters to inches.

   d. A conversion factor for kilometers to miles.

   e. A "straight A" average.

   f. The number of credit hours needed to graduate from your school.

   g. The population of the United States.

   h. The size of an atom.

   i. The distance to the nearest star.

   j. The length of a light year in miles.

   k. The frequency of your favorite radio station.

   l. Your hourly pay rate.

m. The sticker-price of a new automobile.

n. The speed (in revolutions per minute) of a long-playing record album.

Variables

The value of a variable can change during execution of a program. Essentially, a variable represents a storage location where the programmer can cause a value to be stored. To simplify access to these storage locations, the programmer assigns a name to each. The BASIC rule for assigning variable names is quite simple: use any letter of the alphabet (A-Z) or any combination of a single letter followed by a single digit (0-9). Valid variable names include: A, A0, A1, A9, Q, W, X, X1, X6, and so on.

The programmer may select any variable name he or she chooses as long as the syntax rules are followed. It makes sense, however, to select variable names that mean something. For example, P or R would be better names for a pay rate than would L. When computing an average, a variable named A (or M, for mean) would make more sense than one named X. This is for the convenience of the programmer; meaningful variable names make it easier to follow the logic of the program. The computer really doesn't care.

EXERCISES:

1. Which of the following variable names are legal? Which are illegal, and why? Note: $\emptyset$ is the digit zero.

a. R7	d. 6X	g. B13	j. XX
b. QB7	e. Z	h. C8	k. HI
c. I	f. J$\emptyset$	i. 0$\emptyset$	l. a5

Operators

Arithmetic operations in BASIC are defined by using the following operators:

+	addition
–	subtraction
*	multiplication
/	division
↑ or **	exponentiation, involution, or raising to a power

Expressions

An expression is a series of one or more variables and/or constants linked by operators. As we'll learn later, an expression can also include subscripted variables and built-in (intrinsic) functions. The programmer specifies the arithmetic steps the computer is to follow by writing expressions.

To add variables A and B, the programmer would code

A + B

To multiply X by 4, the following expression

X * 4

would be coded. The formula for computing the area of a circle is π times the radius squared. A BASIC expression for this formula would be

3.1416 * R ↑ 2

assuming that the variable R represents the radius.

Certain arithmetic operations should not be coded, as they can lead to program failure on many systems. Do not:

1. Divide by zero.

2. Raise zero to the zero power.

3. Raise zero to a negative power.

4. Raise a negative number to a non-integer power.

5. Compute a value that exceeds the upper limit of your computer system.

6. Compute a value that is smaller than the lower limit of your computer system.

Such errors are generally not intentional. If your program quits in the middle and the word *overflow* or *underflow* appears on your terminal, you may well have violated one of these rules.

Before we move on to more complex expressions, we must first discuss the sequence of operations. Consider, for example, the expression

6 + 4 / 2

Is the value of the expression 5, or is it 8? The answer depends on the order in which the operations are performed. The correct answer, in this case, is 8, because BASIC uses the following sequence rules:

1. Exponentiation (involution) comes first.

2. Multiplication and division come second.

3. Addition and subtraction are done last.

In the event of ties (multiplication *and* division in the same expression, for example) the expression is evaluated from left to right.

What if you wanted the addition to be performed first? As is the case in standard algebra, parentheses can be used to indicate a change in the normal order of computation. The value of the expression

(6 + 4) / 2

would be 5. Any steps enclosed within the parentheses are done before steps outside the parentheses. Note that the normal sequence rules—exponentiation, multiplication/division, addition/subtraction—are followed within a set of parentheses.

Consider, for example, the following expression:

1 + 2 * 3 / 2 ↑ 2

Exponentiation is done first; the expression is thus reduced to:

1 + 2 * 3 / 4

Next comes multiplication. Why is multiplication done before division? Simply because, in the event of ties, computation goes from left to right. We have now reduced the problem to:

1 + 6 / 4

Division comes next; it should be clear that the value of this expression is 2.5.

What if parentheses are used to change the order of computation? The expression:

(1 + 2) * 3 / 2 ↑ 2

is equal to 2.25, but the expression:

(1 + 2 * 3) / 2 ↑ 2

is equal to 1.75, and:

1 + (2 * 3 / 2) ↑ 2

is equal to 10. Why? Just do the computations enclosed within the parentheses first, and you should arrive at the same answers.

It is possible to code one set of parentheses within another; this is called *nesting*. For example, the value of:

$$((1 + 2) * (3 / 2)) \uparrow 2$$

is the same as:

$$(3 \quad * \quad 1.5) \uparrow 2$$

which is 20.25. Compute the value of the *inner* parentheses first. Most versions of BASIC allow for at least three levels of parentheses; some allow as many as seven. Check the reference manual for the limit on your system.

It is strongly recommended that you use parentheses when writing arithmetic expressions. Consider, for example, the expression to compute the area of a circle:

$$3.1416 * (R \uparrow 2)$$

Are the parentheses needed? No. Exponentiation would be done first even if they had not been coded. The parentheses, however, do not hurt, and the intent of the programmer is much more clearly indicated than it would have been had they not been used. *When in doubt, parenthesize.*

Occasionally, parentheses *must be* used. For example, the expression:

$$X * -4$$

is illegal; it should be written as:

$$X * (-4)$$

Under most versions of BASIC, you cannot code two successive operators unless they are separated by a left parenthesis.

You may have noticed that, in the examples cited above, variables, constants, and operators were separated by spaces (blank characters). Blank spaces are not required by BASIC; in fact, they may be ignored by your compiler. They were coded for the convenience of the programmer, simply to make the expression easier to read.

EXERCISES:

1. Write BASIC expressions for the following algebraic expressions:

    a. x+y+2z+8

    b. 2a + 4b + 4c − 2d

c. $\dfrac{x + y}{a + b}$

d. $\dfrac{-b + \sqrt{b^2 - 4ac}}{2a}$

e. $xy - 2x^2 y^2 + 3x^3 y^3$

f. $\dfrac{a}{3} + \dfrac{b^2}{4} - \dfrac{c^3}{3}$

g. $abcd/wxyz + 18.5$

Note that each algebraic variable is a single letter.

2. Find, and code in BASIC, formulas for the following:

a. The area of a triangle.

b. The volume of a cube.

c. The volume of a sphere.

d. The volume of a right circular cylinder.

e. A baseball player's batting average.

f. A baseball pitcher's earned run average.

g. A grade point average.

h. The interest earned on a savings account (assume 5% interest).

3. Given that I=1, J=2, and K=3, find the value of the following BASIC expressions:

a. I + J / 4 + K

b. (I + J) * (K + 2) / J

c. I * J * K / 3

d. (I + J + K) / 3

e. I ↑ J * K

f. I + J + K ↑ 2

g. (I + J + K) ↑ 2

h. $K \uparrow J \uparrow 2$

i. $I + J / I + K$

j. $(I + J) / (I + K)$

STRING EXPRESSIONS

Constants

A *string constant* is a non-numeric constant. String constants may not be used in computations. Basically, they are used to identify or clarify output—printing column headers, for example. Occasionally, the BASIC programmer will have need to test or perform logic on a string constant.

A string constant, sometimes called a *literal constant*, is coded by typing a series of characters enclosed within a set of quotation marks. For example,

"THIS IS A STRING CONSTANT"

You may include as few as one character between the quote marks. Normally, the constant should not extend beyond the length of a single line on your terminal (although some systems do allow the programmer to extend a constant over several lines). Virtually any character that can legally be typed through your keyboard can be included in a literal constant, including lower case letters. The only exception is the quote mark itself. Do *not* try to include a quote mark as part of a literal or string constant, as the quote mark is used to indicate the beginning or the end of such constants. (If you must indicate a quotation within the constant, use the single quote or apostrophe.)

Variables

String variables are used to hold non-numeric information. A string variable is identified by a single letter of the alphabet followed by a dollar sign ($). For example, A$, B$, C$, and Z$ are valid string variables names.

The number of characters that can be stored under a string variable depends on the computer system being used. Some limit the programmer to a single character unless a special instruction (STRING or DIM, for example) has been coded to explicitely set the length of the variable; we'll cover such instructions later. On other systems, the default length is 16 to 18 characters. Still others set the length of a string based on the length of the first constant assigned to it. Upper limits range from the high teens, through about 72 characters, and occasionally as high as 255 characters. Check the BASIC manual for the limits and defaults on your system.

1.   Code a set of string constants containing your name, your address, your zip code, and your telephone number.

2.   Code a string constant to hold your social security number. Why can't you use a numeric constant or variable to hold your social security number?

STATEMENTS

Each step in a BASIC program is defined by coding a statement. A BASIC statement consists of a *statement number*, a command (LET, INPUT, PRINT, END), and a set of operands.

Every BASIC statement must be preceeded by a statement number. Statement numbers (or line numbers) are integer values ranging (in minimal BASIC) from a low of 1 to a high of 9999. Some versions of BASIC allow line numbers greater than 9999. Check the reference manual for the limits set by your system.

The statement number must be followed by at least one blank, after which the command is coded. One or more blanks separate the command from the operands.

The LET Statement

A LET statement is used to assign a constant, the current value of a variable, or the value of an expression to another variable. Do *not* code:

        30   LET   8 = A

It is illegal to code a constant to the left of the equal sign; a single variable must separate the command and the equal sign.

The equal sign (=) in a BASIC LET statement may not mean exactly what you think it does. Consider, for example, the statement:

        60   LET   C = C + 1

Clearly, equating C to C + 1 is a violation of the rules of algebra. A better interpretation of the BASIC statement shown above is: "Assign the value of the expression C + 1 to the variable C." It is legal, and quite common, in BASIC.

Some versions of BASIC support a multiple assignment statement. Assume, for example, that two variables are to be set equal to zero at the beginning of a program. The statements:

        10   LET   A = 0

        20   LET   C = 0

will always work, but on some systems:

        10 LET A = C = 0

is legal. Check your reference manual.

The INPUT Statement

An INPUT statement is used to obtain values for one or more variables from the terminal. For example, coding:

        40 INPUT X, Y, Z

represents a request for values for three different variables. In response to a prompt (a question mark, greater than symbol, etc.) the programmer will be expected to enter the three values.

The rules for entering values vary significantly from system to system. Some, for example, accept only a single value at a time. On such a system, the statement:

        50 INPUT A, B

will be followed by a prompt, the input of a value for A, a second prompt, and the input of a value for B. What if the programmer enters values for both A and B on the first line? The second value might well be ignored. Your instructor will know how your system works.

In many cases, it is better to write a program to request only a single value at a time. Assume, for example, that a payroll program requires the input of an hourly pay rate and hours worked. If both are listed in the same INPUT statement, the programmer must remember which comes first. Often, this problem can be eliminated by requesting one value at a time with a prompting message. For example, the instructions:

        40 PRINT " ENTER HOURS WORKED ";

        50 INPUT H

will cause a message to be printed on the terminal. The semicolon ending the message will cause the prompt associated with the INPUT statement to be printed on the same line. Now, the value to be input is obvious.

What about data type? The type of a variable listed in an INPUT statement must match type of data entered. In other words, in response to:

        70 INPUT X

the value 25 would be reasonable, but "ABC" would not. Enter non-numeric, string data only in response to a string variable. Must quote marks be used to enclose a string value? No. However, if you want embedded blanks to be retained in your string field, use quote marks.

The PRINT Statement

A PRINT statement is used to send the current value of one or more variables or strings to the terminal, where they are displayed. For example, the statement:

80 PRINT "AVERAGE = ", M

would display the literal string as it appears, followed by the value of the variable M.

BASIC divides the output line or the screen into a series of zones, typically five zones per line. Let's assume that the width of a line is 80 characters. With five zones, each would occupy 16 character positions. In the PRINT statement shown above, the string constant "AVERAGE = ' would be displayed starting with the first character in the first zone (Fig. A.1). The comma (,) means "skip to the beginning of the next zone". Thus, the value of M would be displayed starting with character position 17. The result is shown in Fig. A.1.

In the example of Chapter 2, we coded:

130 PRINT "AVERAGE = "; M

What does the semicolon do? Basically, the semicolon means "ignore the zone convention". The result is that one or two spaces are skipped after the literal constant is printed, and the value of M is printed quite close to the first field (Fig. A.2). The rule is quite simple. A comma means skip to the next zone, while a semicolon means to ignore the zone convention and skip a position or two between fields. Your reference manual should describe the zone conventions of your system. If you can't find it, a little experimentation should do just as well.

The IF Statement

An IF statement is used to compare two expressions (variables, constants, or a full-fledged expressions). The conditions that can be tested were listed in Chapter 2, on page 27.

A few cautions are in order. Although many versions of BASIC allow the programmer to use any of the tests on string expressions, many do not. It is suggested that you stay with equal (=), less than (<), or greater than (>) when testing strings.

It is important that when comparing strings you compare fields of equal length. On many systems, the constants "ABC" and "ABC   " are different. The constants " XYZ" and "XYZ   " are different on most.

Consider also the collating sequence. A is always less than B, which in turn is less than Z; the letters of the alphabet will be in the anticipated order. Likewise, 1 is always less than 2, which is less than 3, and so on. How does the digit 1 compare with the letter A, however? On some systems, the digit is larger; on others, the letter is larger. Check the reference manual carefully before comparing mixed string fields.

Do not compare a string and a numeric expression. Compare numbers with numbers and strings with strings. When testing numbers, be very careful of possible

Fig. A.1: *PRINT zones.*

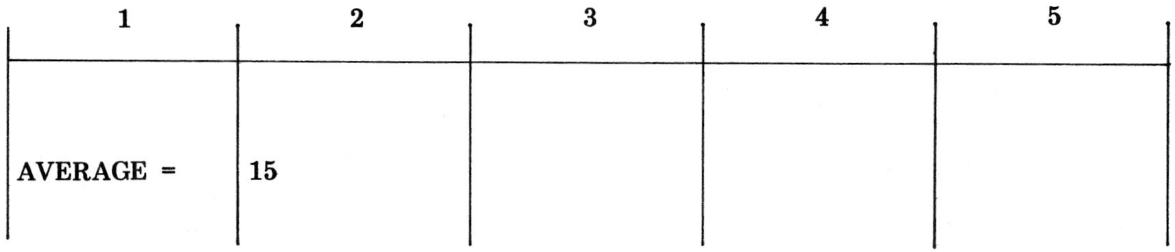

1   2   3   4   5

AVERAGE = | 15

Fig. A.2: *The semicolon means "ignore the zone convention."*

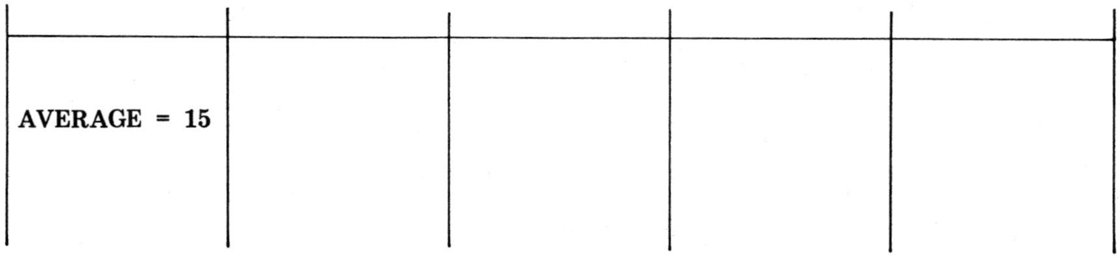

AVERAGE = 15

tolerance errors within your computer. Assume, for example, that you have set up a loop, and that you wish to exit the loop as soon as the value of variable X is equal to 100. You might be tempted to code:

120   IF   X = 100   THEN   200

It is possible, however, that X may *never* equal 100. Instead, X may equal 99.9999 or 100.001, neither of which is *exactly* equal to 100, and the test coded in statement number 120 tells the program to branch only if X is *exactly* equal to 100. Less-than-or-equal-to or greater-than-or-equal-to tests are wise when comparing numbers.

EXERCISES:

If you have not already done so, return to Chapter 2, page 36, and begin writing some programs.

3

Branching
and Looping:
Simple Loops

OVERVIEW

There is an elementary truism in the field of computer programming: The only way to learn to program is to program. We have covered many of the elements of the BASIC language; now, it is time to put our knowledge to work. In this chapter we will plan and code two programs, each involving repetitive logic—a loop. One program will compute the sum of a series of integers. The second will generate a metric-to-English conversion table. Only two new BASIC functions will be introduced: the FOR. . .NEXT loop and the TAB function.

LOOPS

It makes very little sense to write a computer program to find the area of a single circle or the average of a half dozen numbers. Programming takes time. Frankly, it is easier to solve a small problem on a pocket calculator than to write a program to solve it.

Why then do we write programs? Not all problems are small. Although the calculator is fine for computing the area of a single circle, a person assigned the task of computing the areas of all circles with integer radii ranging from 1 to 1000 centemeters would soon grow tired of pushing buttons. When a set of logic, even simple logic, must be repeated many times, it makes sense to take the time to carefully define that logic once, in the form of a computer program. Given a program, it is possible to instruct the computer to execute the logic over and over again, automatically. This is the real advantage of the computer. Repetitive logic need be defined only *once*. By placing this logic in a **loop**, it can be executed as often as necessary.

Most programs involve setting up one or more loops. A loop is a set or series of instructions. It has a clearly defined beginning and a clearly defined end; for example, in the average program, the loop began with an INPUT statement and ended with a GOTO. The idea is simple. Start at the beginning, execute the instructions in the loop in sequence, and then go back to the beginning and do it again.

The idea of repetitive logic, however, is not the whole story. Consider, for example, the following loop:

```
70  LET  N = N + 1

80  GOTO  70
```

Clearly something is missing. It is possible to enter the loop by executing statement number 70, but once in, there is no way out! This is called an **endless loop**, and it's a common beginner's error.

To be valid, every loop must have an exit, a way out. There are many different ways to construct a loop exit. In the average problem, we tested for an end of data condition, exiting the loop when the input value was negative. As an alternative, if the number of times a loop must be repeated is known, we can simply count, leaving the loop when the counter reaches the critical value. Consider instead a problem in which the objective is to find some critical value; for example, how many integers must we add until the sum exceeds 1000? Here, the loop will be executed until the critical value is reached.

In this chapter, we'll be writing two programs, each involving a loop that is controlled by a counter. In Chapter 4, two programs requiring somewhat more complex loop structures will be coded.

A "COUNT" LOOP: THE SUM OF A SERIES OF INTEGERS

What is the sum of the integers from 1 to 200? More generally, what is the sum of the integers from 1 to some unknown upper limit, X? In an algebra course, you may have been exposed to a formula for computing this sum directly. A program using this formula will be more efficient (better!) than a program that sets up a loop to sum the integers, but, for purposes of illustration, we are going to set up a loop anyway.

Ignoring the formula, how would you go about finding the sum of a series of integers? You might begin with a very simple example. If X = 5, the sum of the integers from 1 to X is 1 + 2 + 3 + 4 + 5. Adding two terms at a time generates the following accumulations: 1 + 2 is 3; 3 + 3 is 6; 6 + 4 is 10; 10 + 5 is 15. The sum of the integers from 1 to 5 is 15. A few more simple examples should establish the pattern.

Now, it's time to define the logic. Essentially, finding the sum of a series of integers involves counting and adding. The key steps are:

1. Add the counter to the accumulator.

2. Add 1 to the counter.

3. If the counter is less than or equal to the limit, X, repeat the first two steps.

What about the initial values? What is X? Where should we start the counter and the accumulator? We are, after all, trying to develop a computer program, and we know that the computer assumes nothing; thus, we might define:

1. Initialize X, the upper limit.

2. Initialize the accumulator to zero.

3. Initialize the counter to 1.

Now the main program loop can be entered:

4. Add the counter to the accumulator.

5. Add 1 to the counter.

6. Is the counter less than or equal to X?

7. If yes, go back to statement number 4.

What happens after the loop has been executed the desired number of times? We are ready to print our results and end the program, thus:

8. Print X and the accumulated sum.

9. Stop.

Putting all these steps together, we can now draw the flowchart of Fig. 3.1.

What variables will we need? First, we'll need a variable to hold the upper limit; let's call that X. A counter will be needed; N will do nicely. Finally, an accumulator, A, will be needed to hold the sum of the integers. Our planning is now complete; the BASIC program can be written.

Incidentially, before we continue, you should know that the program we have planned is not the *only* possible solution to this problem. Earlier, we discussed using a simple equation to find the sum of a series of integers, and that algorithm would certainly represent an excellent way to solve this problem. We might choose to control our loop differently, too. Why not, for example, start the counter at X and *subtract* 1 each time through the loop until the counter reaches zero? Other, equally valid solutions are possible.

Writing the "Integers" Program in BASIC

We already know all the instructions we need to write this program. The first three logic blocks can be coded as:

```
70  INPUT  X

80  LET  A = 0

90  LET  N = 1
```

(Statements 10 through 60 will hold the usual start-of-program remarks).

Next, the loop can be written. It's a very simple loop, consisting of only three instructions:

```
100  LET  A = A + N

110  LET  N = N + 1

120  IF  N < = X  THEN  100
```

Finally, the output can be obtained and the program ended:

```
130  PRINT  X,A

140  END
```

That's about it. Once the planning is finished, coding is (and should be) relatively simple.

There is, however, one more point to consider before we leave this program. The loop coded above essentially counts from 1 to some upper limit, exiting the loop when this limit is reached. This sequence is so common in programming, that most languages contain special instructions to simplify the coding of such loops. BASIC is no exception. In BASIC, a simple "count" loop can be defined by coding a **FOR. . .NEXT** loop.

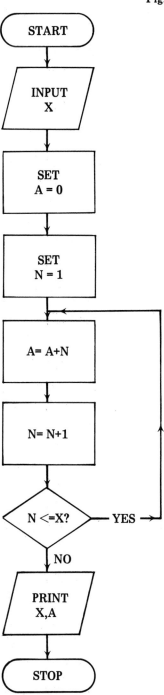

Fig. 3.1: *Flowchart for a program to compute the sum of the integers from 1 to X.*

Fig. 3.2 shows the loop we just ended on the left and an equivalent FOR. . .NEXT loop on the right. The FOR statement defines the top of the loop; the NEXT statement defines the bottom. As the loop begins, the control variable, in this case, N, is set equal to the initial value (1 in this example). The instructions contained within the loop are then executed. When the NEXT statement is encountered, the control variable, N, is incremented "STEP 1". If N is less than or equal to the upper limit (defined by "TO X"), logic returns to the top of the loop; if not, control passes to the first statement following the loop. The general format of a FOR. . .NEXT loop is:

statement no. FOR variable = initial TO limit STEP increment

$\left.\rule{0pt}{20pt}\right\}$ other statements

statement no. NEXT variable

What is the difference between the two loops of Fig. 3.2? Obviously, the FOR. . .NEXT loop requires one less instruction, but that is only a surface difference. Without the FOR. . .NEXT structure, we coded the instructions to initialize, increment, and test the control variable, along with the other instructions in the loop. Most of our code was concerned with controlling the loop, and *not* with performing the primary function of the loop. With the FOR. . .NEXT structure, the loop controls are implied. In effect, the FOR statement defines the start of the loop and the NEXT statement defines the end of the loop. We can concentrate on what the loop is really designed to do; the loop controls do not "clutter" our logic. That is the big advantage of FOR. . .NEXT loops.

Fig. 3.2: *A comparison of two equivalent loop structures.*

the old way	with FOR. . .NEXT statements
90 LET N = 1	90 FOR N = 1 TO X STEP 1
100 LET A = A + N	100 LET A = A + N
110 LET N = N + 1	110 NEXT N
120 IF N < = X THEN 100	

A version of the integer program using a FOR. . .NEXT loop is shown in Fig. 3.3. Note that the "STEP 1" portion of the FOR statement has not been coded; if the increment is 1, the "STEP" parameter is optional.

What exactly does this program do? It is often very instructive to "play computer" on a simple program like this. By following step by step the computer's reaction to the program statements, it is possible to gain a much better understanding of what the program really means. The steps actually executed by this program for an input value X = 3 are outlined in Fig. 3.4. Use a card or a ruler to underline the "current step" as you follow the program logic.

Fig. 3.3: *The integer problem using a FOR. . .NEXT loop.*

```
 10        REM * PROGRAM TO COMPUTE THE SUM OF
 20        REM * THE INTEGERS FROM 1 TO AN
 30        REM * UNKNOWN LIMIT, X.
 40        REM *    WRITTEN BY: W.S. DAVIS
 50        REM *              1/10/81
 60        REM * * * * * * * * * * * * * * * *
 70 INPUT X
 80 LET A=0
 90 FOR N=1 TO X
100    LET A=A+N
110 NEXT N
120 PRINT X,A
130 END
```

Fig. 3.4: *The step by step execution of the integer program.*

Instruction	X	A	N	
1. INPUT X	3	?	?	
2. LET A = 0	3	0	?	
3. Initialize N to 1	3	0	1	
4. LET A = A + N	3	1	1	
5. Increment N	3	1	2	
6. LET A = A + N	3	3	2	the loop
7. Increment N	3	3	3	
8. LET A = A + N	3	6	3	
9. Increment N	3	6	4	
10. N now exceeds X: terminate				
11. PRINT X,A				

to printer

↓   ↓

3   6

The first step in the program is to input a value for X. Space is set aside to hold this value, and the programmer is asked to type the number on the terminal. As the value is read into the program, it is stored in memory. Note that the values of other variables are still unknown.

The next instruction initializes A, the accumulator. Main memory space is set aside to hold this field, and is initialized to zero.

The loop comes next. First, the control variable, is initialized to 1 (Fig. 3.4, line 3). Following initialization, the LET statement is executed; variable A is now equal to 1. The final step in the first iteration of the loop, identified logically as the NEXT statement, increments the control variable by 1. Note in Fig. 3.4 (line 5) that N is now equal to 2.

Is N greater than X, the upper limit? N is 2; X is 3; the answer is clearly "no". Thus control returns to the top of the loop, and N is once again added to A (Fig. 3.4, line 6); A is now 3. The control variable is incremented once again, and the condition (N > X) is tested. N is 3; X is 3; once again the condition is false. As a result, the loop is repeated yet another time.

The LET statement is executed (Fig. 3.4, line 8). N is incremented (line 9). N now exceeds X; therefore the loop ends. The final instruction executed by the program is the PRINT statement, which sends whatever is currently stored in X and whatever is currently stored in A to the terminal.

Take the time to follow the program logic described above. Understand this example, it is important. If you can follow the logic, you will know what the computer does. If you know what the computer does, you will find it easier to write future programs.

The increment in this loop is 1. What if an increment other than 1 was desired? What if, for example, the problem asked the programmer to find the sum of all the odd integers, 1, 3, 5, 7, . . ., up to some limit, X? The statement:

```
120  FOR  N = 1  TO  X  STEP  2
```

would provide control. What if the increment were subject to change; in other words, what if we wanted the program to sometimes work with increments of 1, sometimes 2, sometimes 3, and so on? We might code:

```
100  INPUT  L,I

120  FOR  K = 1  TO  L  STEP  I
```

followed by additional instructions. In this example, the associated NEXT statement might be:

```
150  NEXT  K
```

The NEXT statement always refers to the control variable.

The initial value can be either a constant or a variable. It doesn't have to be 1, either. For example:

```
200  FOR  C = 10  TO  200  STEP  5
```

is perfectly valid. Many versions of BASIC support the use of a negative increment as well. The statement:

```
130  FOR  R = 50  TO  0  STEP  -5
```

would generate the values 50, 45, 40 . . ., 5,0. This last example is not legal in all versions of BASIC.

Not all versions of BASIC construct a FOR. . .NEXT loop in exactly the same way; a few, for example, use

FOR I = J TO K BY L

Most, however, follow the structure described above.

We'll be using a FOR. . .NEXT loop in writing the second program in this chapter.

ANOTHER COUNT LOOP: A METRIC-TO-ENGLISH CONVERSION TABLE

The United States is gradually converting to the metric system. Over the next several years, we will encounter measurements in both systems, so a conversion from metric-to-English or from English-to-metric will often be necessary. To aid in this conversion, we would like to generate a table showing distances ranging from 1 to 100 kilometers along with the equivalent measurements in feet and miles.

Where do we start? Our first step should be to define the algorithms or conversion factors. One kilometer is equal to how many miles? How many feet? How can we find out? You probably have a science book that contains conversion factors. If not, try a good dictionary. Almost invariably, by looking up the term "meter", you can find a conversion expressing the length of a meter in either feet, or inches, or both. A meter is equivalent to 3.281 feet. A kilometer is simply 1000 meters; if one meter is equal to 3.281 feet, 1000 meters is equal to 3281 feet.

A similar set of computations can be used to develop a factor to convert kilometers to miles. The dictionary tells us that there are 5280 feet per mile. If a kilometer is equal to 3281 feet, then a kilometer must be equal to 3281 feet divided by 5280 feet/mile, which is 0.6214 miles. We now have our two conversions factors, and can compute a few key table values, as follows:

KILOMETERS	FEET	MILES
1	3281	0.6214
50	164,050	31.0700
100	328,100	62.1400

Later, this skeleton table will prove useful in checking our results.

What next? Having defined our conversion factors, we might turn our attention to the variables to be manipulated by our program. We'll need one to represent kilometers—K seems logical. Miles will be represented by M; feet, by F.

Finally, we can define the program logic. Essentially, this program will involve a single loop. The number of kilometers will be initialized to 1. The equivalent number of feet and miles will be computed using the conversion factors developed above;

then the values of K, F, and M will be printed. The number of kilometers will be incremented by 1, and the cycle repeated until K is greater than 100. A flowchart of this logic is shown as Fig. 3.5.

We are not quite ready to begin writing the code, however. Consider the partial table that was prepared a few paragraphs back. The computed values are nicely arranged in columns, with a descriptive header at the top of each column. Where did these headers come from? How did we manage to align the headers and the data?

If you have ever used a typewriter, you probably know something about the tab key. By depressing this key, the type-element or the carriage (depending on the typewriter used) moves to a predetermined spot. If the same tab setting is used for both a header and the data in a column, then the header and the data will be aligned.

Much the same thing can be done in BASIC. One or more **TAB functions** among the list of variables following a PRINT statement will cause printed or displayed output fields to begin at predetermined locations. For example, the statement:

130 PRINT TAB(20), "AVERAGE = "

will cause the literal to be printed or displayed beginning at position 20. The statement:

40 PRINT TAB(10),X; TAB(20),Y; TAB(30),Z

will result in three values being displayed, starting with positions 10, 20, and 30 respectively.

How does a programmer go about laying out a reasonable format for a table? The secret lies in knowing the "worst case" for any given column. Most versions of BASIC carry numeric values to six digits of accuracy. Including a decimal point means that seven characters will be needed to represent the data item on output. The numbers in the table will consume no more than seven positions.

Are any of the headers bigger than seven characters? "KILOMETERS" is 10 characters long; thus the first column will need at least ten positions. The other headers are less than seven characters long, so seven positions are more than enough for column 2 and for column 3.

Given these "worse case" conditions, it is easy to plan a layout that will allow us to print all three columns without any overlapping. Several alternatives are possible. We might code the following statement to print our headers.

60 PRINT TAB(5), "KILOMETERS"; TAB(20), "FEET"; TAB(30), "MILES"

When this statement is executed, "KILOMETERS" will be printed or displayed starting at position 5, "FEET" will start with position 20, and "MILES" will start with position 30. Later, inside the loop, the instruction:

100 PRINT TAB(9),K; TAB(20),F; TAB(30),M

Fig. 3.5: *A flowchart of the metric conversion table program.*

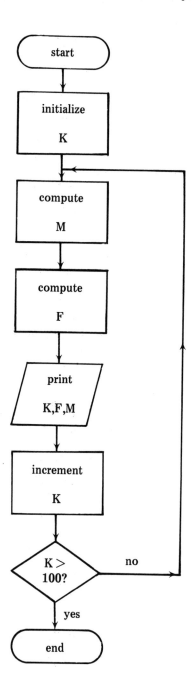

will cause the computed values to be printed under the appropriate header. (Note: we used position 9 to *center* the values for kilometers.) The result will be an attractive, easy-to-read table.

When the TAB function is used, should the items following the PRINT be separated by commas or by semicolons? As you may recall from Chapter 2, the use of a semicolon causes the values in the list to be printed more closely together. Doesn't the TAB function, which specifies the position where a field is to begin, override any other assumptions that BASIC might make as to output spacing? On many versions of BASIC, yes. On other versions, it does make a difference. Since the semicolon means "ignore the print zones standard", semicolons can almost always be used. We have treated the TAB function and its associated variable or literal as a single entity, and separated them with a comma. Before starting a new TAB/variable or TAB/literal set, however, a semicolon was used. This approach is safe on most versions of the language.

Now we can write the BASIC program (Fig. 3.6) using the TAB function. You should have very little trouble following the logic.

How would you go about testing this program? One suggestion is to change the FOR statement (number 70 in Fig. 3.6) to:

70 FOR K = 1 TO 100 STEP 10

This way, key values can be computed and checked, and if anything is wrong, corrections can be made without waiting for a full set of 100 incorrect answers to print out. Following verification, statement 70 can be changed back, and the program run.

Fig. 3.6: *The Conversion table program.*

```
 10                          REM * PROGRAM TO CONVERT KILOMETERS
 20                          REM * TO FEET AND MILES
 30                          REM *    WRITTEN BY: W.S. DAVIS
 40                          REM *              1/10/81
 50                          REM * * * * * * * * * * * * * * * *
 60 PRINT TAB(5),"KILOMETERS";TAB(20),"FEET";TAB(30),"MILES"
 70 FOR K=1 TO 100
 80    LET M=K*.6214
 90    LET F=K*3281
100    PRINT TAB(9),K;TAB(20),F;TAB(30),M
110 NEXT K
120 END
```

SUMMARY

In this chapter we wrote two programs, both involving count-controlled loops. The first program was designed to compute the sum of the integers from 1 to an unknown upper limit, X. A solution was carefully planned, flowcharted, and then coded. A count loop is very common in programming. BASIC includes a FOR. . .NEXT loop structure to make the coding of such loops easier. We introduced the FOR. . .NEXT loop and then recoded the integer problem using this structure. Finally, we followed an imaginary computer step by step as it excuted the program.

A second program called for the creation of a metric-to-English conversion table, comparing kilometers with feet and miles. First, the algorithms were developed and a solution to the problem was planned; then the BASIC code was written. The only new BASIC feature was the TAB function, which allowed us to instruct the program to print the table in neat columns complete with column headers.

EXERCISES

1.   Write a program to compute and print the areas of a series of circles with radii ranging from 1 to 25 in increments of 1.

2.   In Chapter 1, problem number 8, you were asked to develop a flowchart for a program to generate a temperature conversion table. Write this program now.

3.   Chapter 1, exercise 6 presented another problem that you can now code. If an individual is paid 1 cent today, 2 cents tommorrow, 4 cents the day after, and so on (the amount doubles each day), how much money would that person have after 30 days?

4.   Since 1 kilometer equals 1093.6 yards and 0.5396 nautical miles, add these two computations to the distance table program developed in the text. The program should list kilometers, feet, miles, yards, and nautical miles for each value of kilometers from 1 to 100.

5.   The factorial of an integer is defined as the product of that integer and all positive integers less than it. For example,

$$10! = 10x9x8x7x6x5x4x3x2x1$$

and $4! = 4x3x2x1.$

By definition, $1! = 1$ and $0! = 0$. Write a program to compute and print the factorial of an unknown integer; in other words, input the integer, compute its factorial, and print the answer.

6. Assume that an amount of money invested in a savings account earns interest at an annual rate of 5½ percent. The amount of money would represent a beginning balance. The interest earned during the first year would be 5½% of this figure. The ending balance would be the sum of the beginning balance and the interest earned. As we moved into the second year, this new balance would become the beginning balance for computing the interest earned during the second year. Write a program to read an initial amount invested; then develop a table showing the beginning balance, interest earned, and ending balance for each of ten years. You might then generalize your program by reading both an interest rate and the number of years, along with the amount to be invested.

7. Input a number. Then compute and print the first ten powers of this number. It is possible that, if your number is big enough, your computer system will not be able to compute the tenth power. See if you can discover where this overflow condition occurs.

8. An instructor wants to develop a grade conversion table to help translate hour exam grades into a part of a final grade. The hour exam counts 25 percent of the final grade. If a student scores 100 on the exam, he or she will get 25 grade points. An 80 is worth 20 grade points; a 50 is worth 12.5, and so on. Write a program to develop a list of grade point equivalents for grades ranging from a high of 100 to a low of 40, assuming the 25% grade factor. Now, generalize the program to develop a similar list given any percentage grade factor.

9. Write a program to compute the sum of the integers from an unknown lower limit, L1, to an unknown upper limit, L2.

10. Write a program to compute the sum of the *odd* integers from 1 to an unknown upper limit.

11. On the moon, a human being would weigh 16% of his or her earth weight. On Jupiter, this figure would jump to 264%. On Venus, 85% would be the figure; on Mars, a somewhat smaller planet, you would weigh only 38% of your earth weight. Write a program comparing earth weight to the equivalent weight on each of these planets for weights ranging from 50 pounds to 250 pounds in increments of 10.

12. One technique for computing the depreciation of a piece of equipment or a building is the sum-of-the-years'-digits method. For example, assume that an item is expected to last for 5 years. The sum of the years' digits would be $1 + 2 + 3 + 4 + 5$, which is 15. During the first year, 5/15 of the value of the asset would be depreciated; during the second year, 4/15 would be depreciated, and so on, until, during the fifth year, the remaining 1/15 would be depreciated. Write a program to input the value of an asset and the estimated life of this asset and then print a depreciation schedule showing the amount depreciated for each year of life.

13. Write a program to accumulate the series: $1+1/2 + 1/3 + 1/4 + 1/5 + \ldots + 1/100$. Print the answer.

Branching
and Looping:
More Complex Loops

4

OVERVIEW

In Chapter 3, we planned and coded two programs using a simple counter as the loop control. The programs to be developed in this chapter will require more complex loop structures. The first program will compare the changing populations of two countries. The main loop will be executed repetitively until a critical condition, computed within the loop, is reach. The second program will create a table of wind chill factors using loops similar to the count loops of Chapter 3. The formula for computing a wind chill factor, however, involves two variables: temperature and wind velocity. To control two variables we will need two loops, one inside the other—nested loops.

No new BASIC instructions will be needed for the population program. The concept of BASIC "built-in" functions will be introduced with the second program.

A CRITICAL CONDITION LOOP: POPULATION STATISTICS

In mid-1979, the population of the United States was estimated at 226 million, while Mexico's was estimated at 66 million. The United States had, however, almost reached zero population growth, with an annual growth rate of only 0.9%, while Mexico's population was increasing at a 2.8% rate. Clearly, if the 1979 growth rates were to continue, there might come a time when the population of Mexico would surpass the United States'. Given the growth rates described above, when would this condition be expected to occur? Developing the algorithms is the key to this problem. What do we mean by growth rate? How does the growth rate affect the population? The growth rate is simply a measure of the amount by which a population increases each year. In any given year, some people are born and some die; some people immigrate, and others emigrate. If the number of people added to a population is greater than the number who leave, the growth rate is positive; otherwise it's negative. A growth rate of 2.8% means that Mexico's population increased by this amount during 1979.

Let's use a simple example to develop our algorithms. We'll imagine that a tiny country called Nowhere has a population of 1000 people, with a growth rate of 10%. During the first year of our study, the population will increase by 10% of that 1000 people; in other words, the population *increase* will be 100 people. What will the population of Nowhere be at the end of the year? If we had 1000 at the start, and added a net total of 100, there will be 1100 people at the end of the year. What happens during the second year? We have 1100 as the year starts. The population increases by 10%—110 new people are added. The population at year's end will be 1210. Those 100 people who joined the population during year 1 will have children of their own, or be joined by friends or relatives immigrating from other countries; they contribute to growth, too.

Now, let's generalize. Let X be the population of the country as the year begins. Let "i" be the growth rate. The increase in population for the year will be:

net increase = Xi,

or the product of the population and the growth rate. What will the population be at the end of the year? The sum of the start of year population, X, and the population growth, Xi. Expressed algebraically:

end-of-year population = X + Xi

If you are familiar with algebra, you know that we can factor this relationship to get:

end-of-year population = X(1+i).

What is the population at the beginning of year two? The same as the population at the end of year one; in other words:

$$X = X(1+i)$$

is a relationship for computing the end-of-year population. If this relationship were placed in a loop and executed repetitively, it could start with the population at time zero, compute the population at the end of the first year, then use this new population to find the number of people at the end of the second year, and so on.

The growth rate for the United States (in 1979) was 0.9%. If we let U stand for the population of the U.S., then the BASIC statement:

160   LET   U = U * (1 + 0.009)

or:

160   LET   U = U * 1.009

can be used to compute the expected population of the country in each of a series of years. Likewise, if the growth rate for Mexico were 2.8%, and M represents the population, the statement:

170   LET   M = M * 1.028

can be used to compute the year-by-year population of Mexico. We have our algorithms.

Beyond defining the algorithms, the logic of the program is really quite simple (Fig. 4.1). The populations of the two countries are initialized, and the year is set to (in this example) 1979. Then we enter our loop. The 1980 populations of both Mexico and the United States are computed and compared. If Mexico still has fewer people than the United States, the program returns to the top of the loop, where populations for 1981 are computed and compared. The loop continues until the condition "population of Mexico is less than population of U.S." is no longer true. All that remains is to print the two populations and the year when Mexico moves ahead.

Writing the program should be easy; a version is shown in Fig. 4.2. The only thing that might be confusing is the way the large population numbers are shown. Consider, for example, statement number 130:

130   LET   U=2.26E8

The constant on the right side of the equal sign is displayed in floating-point form. The letter "E" is used to designate the value 10 raised to a power. The constant is, in scientific notation, 2.26×10^8, or 226,000,000—just move the decimal point 8 positions. Most versions of BASIC will use scientific notation to display very large or very small numbers. If you prefer, you could type 226000000; BASIC would convert the number to floating point. As a final note, the printed output (Fig. 4.2) is in floating point form for the population statistics, but the year looks normal. Only very large and very small numbers are converted to floating-point form. How large or how small? That depends on the version of BASIC used. Ask your instructor about your system or, better yet, experiment on your own.

Fig. 4.1: *The logic of the population problem.*

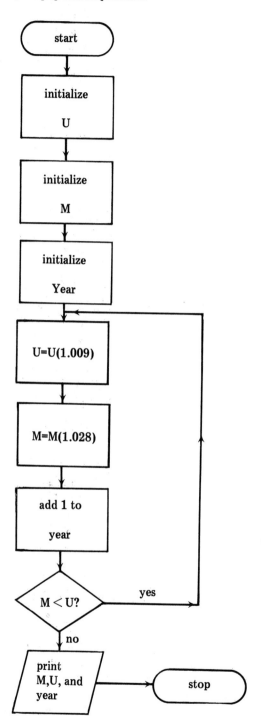

Fig. 4.2: *The population program.*

```
 10                       REM * PROGRAM TO DETERMINE WHEN POPULATION
 20                       REM * OF UNITED STATES AND POPULATION OF
 30                       REM * MEXICO ARE EQUAL.
 40                       REM *    INITIAL CONDITIONS:
 50                       REM *      POP. US      226 MILLION
 60                       REM *      POP. MEXICO   66 MILLION
 70                       REM *      GROWTH, US   0.9%
 80                       REM *      GROWTH, MEX  2.8%
 90                       REM *      YEAR          1979
100                       REM * WRITTEN BY: W.S. DAVIS
110                       REM *           1/10/81
120                       REM * * * * * * * * * * * * * * * * * *
130 LET U=2.26E8
140 LET M=6.6E7
150 LET Y=1979
160 LET U=U*1.009
170 LET M=M*1.028
180 LET Y=Y+1
190 IF M<U THEN 160
200 PRINT "POP. US =";U,"POP. MEX = ";M,"IN";Y
210 END

>run

POP. US = 4.08251E+08     POP. MEX =  4.08407E+08     IN 2045
```

NESTED LOOPS: PREPARING A WIND CHILL FACTOR TABLE

If you live in an area where the winter temperature sometimes drops below thirty degrees, you have probably heard of the wind chill factor. The idea is really quite simple. As anyone who has been out in the cold knows, the degree of discomfort or the risk of frostbite are not only functions of temperature. On a windless day, twenty degrees may be quite comfortable, but when a brisk wind is blowing, that same twenty degrees seems intolerable. Just as the sumertime combination of heat and humidity is worse than the heat alone, the wintertime combination of cold and wind is far worse than just the cold. In fact, this latter combination can be deadly.

The wind chill factor is a number used to measure the combined effect of low temperature and wind. By plugging the temperature (in Fahrenheit) and the wind velocity (in miles per hour) into a formula, an "equivalent temperature" is computed; in theory, this temperature (with no wind) is equivalent to the given combination of temperature and wind. For example, a day on which the temperature is 20 degrees and the wind is blowing at 20 miles per hour will seem as cold as a day when the temperature is minus six degrees and there is no wind.

You may be able to find the formula for computing a wind chill factor in a general science textbook, a text on meteorology, or an encyclopedia. However, it is not generally available; thus, rather than asking you to find it, we'll list it below:

$$WCF = 91.4 - (.288\sqrt{V} + .450 - .019V) * (91.4 - TEMP),$$

where "V" is the wind velocity in miles per hour and "TEMP" is measured in degrees Fahrenheit.

How do you react when faced with such a formula? Many people simply panic when they see all those terms. Don't. Break the formula into pieces; it's much easier to handle that way. We might, for example, use the following steps:

$$W1 = (.288\sqrt{V} + .450 - .019V)$$

$$W2 = (91.4 - TEMP)$$

$$WCF = 91.4 - (W1 * W2)$$

(Using these three simple steps will also decrease the risk of typing errors as we begin to enter our BASIC program.)

Now that we have the algorithm, let's consider how we might structure a program to generate a table of wind chill factors. We would like to pick a temperature, 20 degrees Fahrenheit, for example, and then compute the wind chill factors associated with this temperature in combination with a variety of wind velocities. We might describe this logic as:

1. initialize temperature.

2. initialize wind velocity,

3. compute wind chill factor,

4. print temperature, wind velocity, and wind chill factor,

5. increment to next wind velocity,

6. if wind velocity is less than or equal to the desired upper limit, go back to step number 3.

It's a simple loop, similar in many ways to the count loops of Chapter 3.

What next? Once a series of wind chill factors has been computed for a given temperature, we might want to select another temperature and repeat the loop. Assume, for example, that we want wind chill factors for wind velocities ranging from 10 to 50 miles per hour, and for temperatures from −30 up to 30 degrees Fahrenheit. Of course, we could obtain the desired output by executing the logic described above, then changing the instruction that initializes the temperature and rerunning the program. It would be easier, however, to include the instructions needed to change the value of temperature in the program. Consider, for example, the following logic:

1. initialize temperature,

    2. initialize wind velocity,

    3. compute wind chill factor,

    4. print temperature, wind velocity, and wind chill factor,

    5. increment to next wind velocity,

    6. if wind velocity is less than or equal to the desired upper
        limit, go back to step number 3.

7. increment to next temperature,

8. if temperature is less than or equal to desired upper limit,
    go back to step number 2.

These steps are shown graphically in Fig. 4.3.

Steps 2 through 6 have intentionally been indented to better show their relationship to steps 1, 7, and 8. We have a loop within a loop. The **outer loop** controls the value of temperature. The **inner loop**, which is part of the outer loop, controls the value of the wind velocity. The first time through the outer loop, temperature will be initialized, and then the inner loop will be repeated many times. After the inner loop has been processed the specified number of times, a second cycle of the outer loop begins; once again the inner loop will be repeated several times. The two loops are said to be **nested**.

When two or more loops are nested, one loop is coded *completely* inside another (Fig. 4.4). It is legal to have one loop within another loop, within yet another loop, and so on—multiple levels of nesting. Some versions of BASIC may limit the number of levels of nesting, but on most the only real limit is the programmer's ability to keep track of what is going on. Two "nested" loops may *not* overlap (Fig. 4.4 again).

In general, the structure of the wind chill factor program is shown in Fig. 4.5. Note that two FOR. . .NEXT loops are nested, one to control the temperature, and the other to control the wind velocity. A few new BASIC features must be introduced before the formula can be coded, however.

One term in the wind chill factor formula calls for the square root of V. What exactly is a square root? The square root of V is a number which, when multiplied by itself, gives V. How is a square root computed? Unfortunately, there is no easy way to compute a square root directly; normally, square roots are estimated. How can a BASIC programmer obtain a reasonable estimate of the square root of a number?

Square roots can be estimated in two ways. First, a square root is simply the ½ power of a number; in other words:

X**0.5 or X↑0.5

Fig. 4.3: *The logic of the wind chill factor program.*

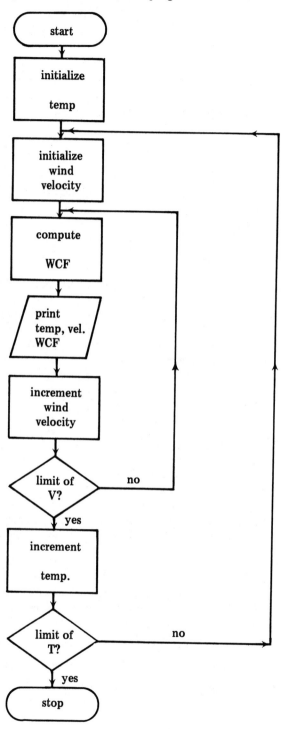

Fig. 4.4: *Nested Loop structures.*

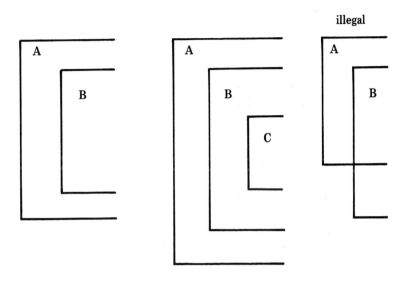

Fig. 4.5: *The structure of the wind chill factor program.*

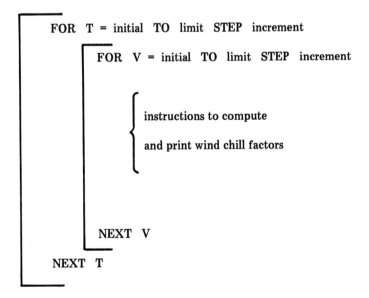

means the same thing as $\sqrt{X}$. In BASIC, writing X↑0.5 will produce an estimate of the square root of X. This technique can be used to find any root of a number. For example, the cube root of X is

X↑(1/3)

and the fourth root is:

X↑0.25   or   X↑(1/4).

Square roots are much more common in mathematical analysis than cube roots or fourth roots. Thus a special **BASIC function** has been developed to provide an accurate estimate of a square root. By coding:

SQR(X)

in an expression, the programmer can take advantage of this built-in function, which is available on most versions of BASIC.

Usually, other functions are available as well. They provide estimates of common trigonometric functions, exponential values, logarithms, absolute values, random numbers, and other commonly used mathematical terms; a list of BASIC functions is provided in Module B, immediately following this chapter. Incidently, TAB is another BASIC function.

Now, we can write the BASIC LET statements for computing a wind chill factor. Using T for the temperature, V for the wind velocity, and W for the wind chill factor, the following three statements will perform the desired computations:

220   LET   W1 = (.288 * SQR(V)) + .45 - (.019 * V)

230   LET   W2 = 91.4 - T

240   LET   W = 91.4 - (W1 * W2)

Generally, wind chill factors are shown as whole numbers. The computed factor for 0 degrees Fahrenheit and a wind velocity of 20 miles per hour is –32.7189 degrees; this would be shown as –33 degrees. How can we convert the fractional numbers generated within the computer to whole number (or integer) form? We can use another BASIC function, the INT function. The expression:

INT(X)

generates the greatest integer that is less than or equal to the argument (in this case, X). Thus, we could code:

250   LET   W = INT(W)

to get this nearest integer.

The INT function does introduce a degree of inaccuracy. In most versions of BASIC, the INT function *truncates* the number; in other words, it drops the fractional portion. *Rounding* might be preferable. The rule for rounding says to add 1 to the units position if the fractional value is greater than or equal to .5. In the example cited on the previous page (−32.7189), the fractional portion is greater than .5, and thus −33 is the preferred answer. How can we round numbers in BASIC?

With positive values, the answer is easy. Suppose that X is a positive number. The expression:

INT(X+0.5)

would generate the value of X rounded to the nearest integer. Why? Consider the following table:

X	X+0.5	INT(X+0.5)
1.3	1.8	1
1.5	2.0	2
1.7	2.2	2

See how it works? Adding 0.5 has no impact on the integer value if the fractional part is less than 0.5, but forces the value to the next highest integer if the fractional portion is greater than or equal to 0.5.

With negative values, the answer is more difficult. Technically, adding −0.5 and then using the INT function should generate the nearest integer, but this doesn't work on all versions of BASIC. Experiment with your version; adding either 0.5 or −0.5 to a negative number should generate the desired answer. In either case, you will probably have to test for a negative value before rounding. To avoid complicating the textbook example, we will simply accept the truncated value.

A completed version of the wind chill program is shown as Fig. 4.6. You should have little trouble following the logic. Note that a set of column headers is printed (statement number 190) *before* the nested loops begin. Why is the statement to print headers placed here? Note also that the statements comprising the inner loop are clearly indented; in effect, indentation visually defines the loop structure. Some versions of BASIC automatically indent the statements making up a FOR. . .NEXT loop. If yours does not, indent them yourself. Finally, note the use of a PRINT statement followed by "nothing" in statement number 280. Its function is to print a blank line, thus separating the table into temperature groupings. A portion of the output generated by this program is shown as Fig. 4.7.

How would you test the wind chill factor program? Select a few sets of values from the table and do the calculations with a pocket calculator. You should be able to generate approximately the same answers. If not, first check your own computations, then check your algorithms.

Fig. 4.6: *The wind chill factor program.*

```
10  REM * THIS PROGRAM PRINTS A WIND CHILL
20  REM * FACTOR TABLE. GIVEN THE TEMPERATURE
30  REM * AND THE WIND VELOCITY (IN MPH), THE
40  REM * WIND CHILL FACTOR IS COMPUTED FROM
50  REM * A FORMULA. THE FORMULA WILL BE BROKEN
60  REM * INTO 3 SEGMENTS TO SIMPLIFY THE LOGIC
120 REM *     TABLE ENTRIES WILL BE FOR WIND
130 REM *   VELOCITIES RANGING FROM 10 TO 50 MPH
140 REM * AND FOR TEMPERATURES RANGING FROM -30
150 REM * TO 30 DEGREES.
160 REM *        WRITTEN BY: W.S. DAVIS
170 REM *               1/10/81
180 REM * * * * * * * * * * * * * * * * * * * * *
190 PRINT TAB(10),"TEMP";TAB(20),"WIND-MPH";TAB(30),"WCF"
200 FOR T=-30 TO 30 STEP 10
210   FOR V=10 TO 50 STEP 10
220     LET W1=(.288*SQR(V))+.45-(.019*V)
230     LET W2=91.4-T
240     LET W=91.4-(W1*W2)
250     LET W=INT(W)
260     PRINT TAB(10),T;TAB(20),V;TAB(30),W
270   NEXT V
280   PRINT
290 NEXT T
300 END
```

80

Fig. 4.7: *The output from the wind chill factor program.*

TEMP	WIND-MPH	WCF
-30	10	-51
-30	20	-74
-30	30	-86
-30	40	-93
-30	50	-96
-20	10	-40
-20	20	-60
-20	30	-71
-20	40	-77
-20	50	-80
-10	10	-28
-10	20	-47
-10	30	-57
-10	40	-62
-10	50	-65
0	10	-16
0	20	-33
0	30	-42
0	40	-47
0	50	-50
10	10	-4
10	20	-20
10	30	-28
10	40	-32
10	50	-34
20	10	7
20	20	-6
20	30	-13
20	40	-17
20	50	-19
30	10	19
30	20	8
30	30	1
30	40	-2
30	50	-3

SUMMARY

In this chapter, we wrote two programs involving somewhat more-complex loop structures. The first was a population program. The populations and growth rates of Mexico and the United States were given. The question was: When will Mexico's population overtake the United States'?

The program basically involved a loop. Within the loop the populations of the two countries were computed year by year, and then compared. As long as Mexico's population was less than that of the United States, the loop was repeated; as soon as this condition no longer held, the loop was terminated and the answer printed. The key idea was controlling a loop by using values generated within the loop. Actually, the most significant problem faced in this example was defining the algorithms.

The second problem involved nested loops. The program was designed to generate a table of wind chill factors. Once again, defining the algorithm was the first problem. Once the algorithm was defined, we turned to the structure of the program, describing it as a loop within a loop. We discovered that a number of BASIC functions can be used to simplify coding certain operations: SQR, INT, and TAB were used.

EXERCISES

1.   Add to the chapter example that computed a table of wind chill factors, the logic needed to round to the nearest integer.

2.   Given the populations and growth rates of the first example, estimate the combined populations of the United States and Mexico in the year 2000.

3.   Once again using the populations and growth rates of the first example, in what year will the population of the United States be expected to pass 300 million?

4.   Modify the wind chill factor program so that it generates a table for temperatures from -20 to 40 degrees, and wind velocities ranging from 5 to 50 MPH in increments of 5.

5.   An individual borrows $1000 and agrees to pay it back in a series of $50 payments. Interest is charged at 1.5 percent per month on the unpaid balance. The first few payments might be summarized as follows:

Month	Beginning Balance	Total Payment	Interest	Principle	Ending Balance
1	1000.00	50.00	15.00	35.00	965.00
2	965.00	50.00	14.48	35.52	929.48
3	929.48	50.00	13.94	36.06	893.42

Note that the beginning balance for any given month is the same as the ending balance for the preceeding month. Note also that the interest is always 0.015 times the beginning balance, and the amount credited to interest is always $50.00 minus the amount of interest.

Write a program to list this table until the ending balance is zero.

6. Generalize problem number 6 to input the amount of the loan, the monthly payment, and the interest rate. Then generate a month-by-month table until the ending balance is zero.

7. One technique for estimating the square root of a number is based on Newton's method. The programmer provides an initial "guess" of the square root. This guess (x) is then plugged into the formula:

$$EST = 0.5 * (X + (T/X)),$$

where: EST is the new estimate,

X is the "first guess" or a prior estimate,

T is the number whose square root you wish to find,

yielding a new estimate of the square root. This new estimate is then substituted for X in the formula, and another new estimate is generated. This process continues until the answer is "close enough". How can the program tell when this condition is met? If the value of:

$$ABS \left[\frac{X - EST}{X} \right]$$

is less than a very small value selected by the programmer (0.0001 for example), the degree of error in the estimate is said to be close enough.

Write a program to input T, the number whose square root is to be found, and X, an initial estimate. Use Newton's method to estimate the square root.

8. Add to program number 7 the instructions needed to compute and print the square root of T as generated by T**0.5 and as generated by SQR(T), along with your own estimate. Compare the results.

9.   A technique for integration easily applied to the computer involves dividing the area under any curve into a series of rectangles, computing the area of each rectangle, and then summing the areas. Initially, the area might be divided into two rectangles, then four, eight, sixteen, and so on. With each cycle, the sum of the areas of the triangles will be closer and closer to the actual area under the curve. Write a program to integrate the area under a curve using this technique. Make up your own function, or use $Y = 1.5 \; X^2$, for values of X between 1 and 10. Define an acceptable solution as one for which the "prior" estimate and the "new" estimate differ by less than 0.01%.

10.   Using combinations of half-dollars, quarters, nickels, dimes, and pennies, how many different ways can one make change for a dollar?

11.   Write a program to generate a multiplication table.

12.   Write a program to make change. Read the amount of a purchase and the amount paid; the difference is the amount of change due the customer. (Be careful, it may be negative.) Print the total amount of change due and list the composition of this change: i.e., how many dollars, half-dollars, nickels, dimes, quarters, and pennies should be given to the customer?

13.   Write a program to generate a sales tax table. Start with a purchase of 10 cents, and assume a tax of 1 cent on this amount. Given a tax rate of 5%, increment the amount of the purchase 1 cent at a time and compute the amount of tax due on this new amount. As soon as the computed amount of tax *exceeds* 1 cent, you have located the lower bound of the next tax bracket. Print 10 cents, the value one less than the critical point you have just discovered, and the amount of the tax—1 cent. Now, using the just computed critical point as a lower bound, find the point at which the computed tax exceeds 2 cents; this defines the lower bound of the next tax bracket. Print the lower and upper bounds and the tax amount. Continue until the amount of the sale reaches $10.00.

14.   Earlier, you wrote a program to compute the value of the $24 the Indians were paid for Manhatten Island, had they invested their money; the formula is:

$$P = 24 \; (1 + i)^n,$$

where i is the interest rate and "n" is the number of years. Use 8.5% interest; the property was sold in 1626. Show the value of the money at 50 year intervals.

15.   The mathematical constant e is the limit of $(1 + 1/n)^n$ as n approaches infinity. Write a program to estimate a value for e. Stop when the difference between two successive estimates is less than 0.0001. Print the values of e and n.

16.   The sine of a number is defined by the formula:

$$\sin x = x - (x^3/3!) + (x^5/5!) - (x^7/7!) \ldots$$

where 3! is the factorial of 3. Write a program to read a value of x and estimate the sine. An acceptable answer is defined as one for which the error is less than 0.01%. Compare your answer with the one generated by the BASIC function SIN(X).

17. "It's not the heat, it's the humidity." This common summer-time complaint recognizes that the discomfort an individual feels is due to the humidity as well as the heat. In fact, there is a measure of this degree of discomfort analogous to the wind chill factor. The temperature/humidity index is computed from the formula:

$$THI = TEMP - (0.55 - 0.55RH)(TEMP - 58),$$

where TEMP is in degrees Fahrenheit, and RH is the relative humidity in decimal form (60% is .60).

Write a program to create a table of temperature/humidity indexes for temperatures ranging from 70 degrees to 110 degrees and for relative humidities ranging from 60% to 100%. Use increments of 5 in both cases.

Module B

BASIC
Built-in Functions

Certain mathematical terms are encountered with such frequency that special built-in functions have been developed to compute or estimate them. This module describes the functions that are commonly available in BASIC.

AN EXAMPLE

Assume that a BASIC program is to compute value of the following algebraic equation:

$$c = \sqrt{a^2 + b^2}$$

Some of you may recognize this as the formula for computing the length of the third side of a triangle, given the other two. A BASIC LET statement to perform these computations would be:

120 LET C = SQR(A↑2 + B↑2)

SQR is a *built-in function*. The expression enclosed in parentheses is called the *argument*. Essentially what happens is that the value of the argument is computed (do what is enclosed within the parentheses first). Then the value of the argument is passed to the square root function, and the root is estimated. The result in effect replaces the reference to the SQR function. Finally, in this example, the estimated square root will be stored at variable C.

All the built-in functions are used in much the same way; simply code the function name followed by an argument enclosed in a set of parentheses. The argument can be a constant, a variable, or an expression. It can even contain a reference to another built-in function. You can use built-in functions in much the same way that you use constants or variables in building an expression.

Note that you cannot code:

150 LET SQR(X) = 25

The built-in function is *not* a variable, so it cannot be coded to the left of the equal sign in a LET statement.

A TABLE OF COMMON BUILT-IN FUNCTIONS

The following built-in functions are available in most versions of BASIC. In each case, X is used to represent the argument, which may be a constant, a variable, or an expression.

Function	Returns
ABS(X)	The absolute value of the argument.
ATN(X)	The arctangent of the argument. The argument must be expressed in radians.
COS(X)	The cosine of the argument. The argument must be expressed in radians.
EXP(X)	The value of e^X.

INT(X)	The greatest integer which is less than or equal to the argument.
LOG(X)	The natural logarithm of the argument.
RND(X)	Often, simply RND. Returns a random number between 0 and 1.
SGN(X)	Set to -1 if the argument is negative, 0 if the argument is 0, or +1 if the argument is positive.
SIN(X)	The sine of the argument. The argument must be expressed in radians.
SQR(X)	The square root of the argument. Note that the argument may not be negative.
TAB(X)	The value of the argument determines where the next character is to be positioned in an output line. In some versions of BASIC, the argument must be a simple integer constant.
TAN(X)	The tangent of the argument. The argument must be expressed in radians.

5

Structure and Style: Modular Program Design

OVERVIEW

Thus far, the programs we have considered have been relatively simple: most "real world" programs are much more complex. In this chapter we will investigate techniques for dealing with such problems. When faced with a complex programming assignment, the good programmer will often subdivide it into a series of simple modules, attacking each as an independent problem. When these simple modules are combined, a program to solve the more complex problem can be constructed. This modular approach to program design is perhaps the most important single concept that the beginning programmer can learn.

Two new BASIC instructions are needed to support modular program design: GOSUB and RETURN.

PROGRAM COMPLEXITY

Real world problems are frequently quite complex; computer programs tend to reflect this complexity. Consider, for example, the common business data processing problem of computing a payroll. On the surface, the structure of this problem is simple. To compute payroll for any given individual:

1. compute gross pay (generally, the product of hours worked and an hourly pay rate),

2. compute the amount of each deduction, including federal income tax, state income tax, local income tax, social security tax, and others,

3. subtract the deductions from gross pay to get net (takehome) pay.

Where is the complexity? It lies beneath the surface, within the individual, detailed computations.

Gross pay provides a good example. Most of us tend to think of gross pay as a simple computation: if you work for 30 hours, and your pay rate is $5.00 per hour, your gross pay is the product of these two numbers, $150.00. There is much more to it, however. What about overtime? Typically, hours over 40 in any given week are paid at 1½ times the regular rate. What about shift premium? Often, people who work on the night shift receive an extra 8 to 10 percent. How can we handle bonus payments? What about the salesperson who is paid a commission? Managers and other professionals are often paid a salary rather than an hourly wage; how is their pay computed?

These are but a few of the questions that must be answered before the payroll program can be coded. Each of the taxes, and each of the other deductions can be equally complex. The broad structure of the program *is* simple; it is easy to see, in general, what must be done. The detailed computations are complex. Combining a large gross pay routine, a large income tax routine, and several other large computational routines produces a very large (and hence very complex) program. How do professional programmers deal with this complexity?

MODULAR PROGRAMMING: DIVIDE AND CONQUER

The solution is to divide the program into pieces, and then to attack the pieces one at a time. It is relatively easy to write the instructions to compute gross pay, even with all the complicated rules. It is relatively easy to write a program to compute federal income tax. The problem is one of dealing with *all* this complexity at one time. Don't! Solve a series of little problems one at a time; then put the pieces together. This is the essence of modular programming.

Modular program design provides a framework for planning a complex program. We begin by defining, broadly, the function to be performed: in our payroll example, that function is to compute payroll. Now, we can begin to define the specific tasks needed to complete this primary function. In general, to compute payroll we must:

1. read a set of payroll data,

2. compute gross pay,

3. compute social security tax,

4. compute income tax,

5. compute other deductions (we won't list them all),

6. compute net pay,

7. print a paycheck.

These steps will be repeated for each employee. A graphic view of the program as we now see it is shown in Fig. 5.1. This is called a **hierarchy chart**; it shows the relationship between the modules that compose the program.

The module at the top of Fig. 5.1 is called the **mainline** or control module. Its function is to tie together all the second-level routines, controlling the order in which they are executed. The mainline will begin by telling the first of the level-II modules to "read a record". The actual instructions to accomplish the input operation will be found in this second level module. When the task is completed, control is returned to the mainline, which tells the second of the level-II modules to "compute gross pay". Once again, the detailed computations are carried out by this lower-level module; once again control is returned to the mainline. Each secondary routine or **subroutine** is executed in turn, but always under control of the mainline.

What is the advantage of structuring a program this way? Very simply, each subroutine can be written independently. As a result, we can write the code needed to compute gross pay, and then write the code needed to compute income tax without worrying about how the gross pay module was written. If the program becomes too lengthy, we can subdivide responsibility, assigning the subroutines to different programmers. As we shall see, this structure greatly simplifies writing and developing a complex program.

After the program is complete, other advantages accrue. Consider, for example, the problem of locating and fixing a bug. Assume that income tax is being incorrectly computed. Since all the code for computing income tax is contained in a single module, the programmer can ignore the bulk of the program and concentrate on this relatively small routine. Almost immediately the search is narrowed; as a result the bug is easier to find and to correct. This simplification in program "debugging" is a consequence of the structure of the program.

Program maintenance is also greatly simplified. What happens when the federal government passes new laws that change income tax withholding rates? Since all tax computations are found in a single subroutine, the most we will have to do is rewrite that subroutine; the rest of the program can be left as is. What happens when a new union contract changes the rules for computing gross pay? Once again, only one sub-routine is affected. To the student who (typically) writes a program and then discards it at the end of the semester, this ease of maintenance may not seem significant. However, maintenance is a critical concern to the professional programmer who must debug someone else's (bad) code.

Philosophically, modular programming seems to make sense. Let's get more concrete. How can we go about designing and developing a program in modular style? Where do we start?

The mainline is the key to the program: it ties the entire program together. Thus the obvious place to start is with the mainline. Of course, we are not ready to deal with all the details, so we won't. Instead, we will write a **skeleton mainline**, with all functions securely in place, but at a very superficial level.

The Skeleton Mainline

What is a skeleton mainline? Essentially, it's an outline. Like an outline, a skeleton mainline shows the specific steps that will be included in the finished product, and clearly defines the sequence of these steps. The only thing missing is the detail.

Earlier in the chapter, we described the functions that must be performed to compute an individual's pay, including:

1. read a set of payroll data,

2. compute gross pay,

3. compute social security tax,

4. compute income tax,

5. compute net pay,

6. print a paycheck.

In a typical payroll program, other deductions will be involved, but this outline is sufficient for our purposes.

Given this outline, our next task is to define a simple (but realistic) algorithm for implementing each function. Gross pay, for example, is defined as the product of hours worked and an hourly pay rate. Social security tax is simply 6.65 percent of gross pay. Ten percent of gross might represent a reasonable estimate of income tax. Finally, net pay is gross pay minus both social security tax and income tax. Of course these algorithms are not entirely correct. There are merely *dummy* algorithms designed to allow us to write a skeleton mainline.

What about output data? Clearly, if we are to write a paycheck, we must have the employee's name and a computed amount for net pay. We know where net pay comes from—the algorithm we just defined. Where does the name come from? It must come from the first input operation. What other values will be needed on input? Hours

Fig. 5.1: A hierarchy chart of the payroll program.

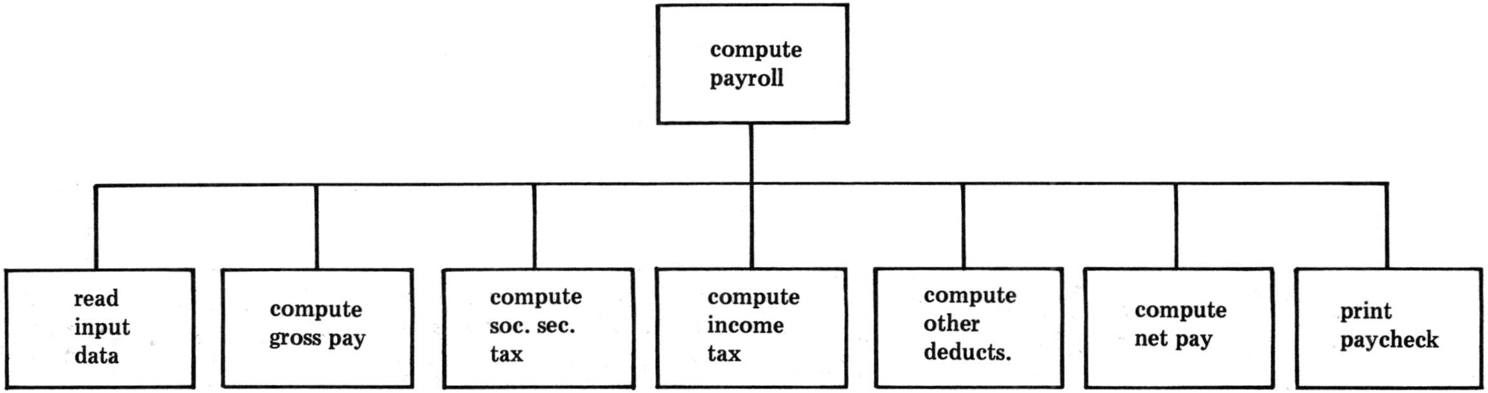

worked and the hourly pay rate must be available before gross pay can be computed, so they must come from the input statement.

A simple flowchart of the skeleton mainline can now be prepared (Fig. 5.2). A program written to implement this logic is shown as Fig. 5.3.

The program of Fig. 5.3 contains only one new BASIC feature. Two of the values that are read into the program are character rather than numeric values—the employee name and initials. **Character variables** are defined by using any letter followed by a dollar sign ($); for example, A$, B$, and so on. Character variables may not be used in arithmetic expressions. It is possible to assign a value to a character variable; for example:

      20 LET C$ = "HELLO"

or:

      70 LET X$ = Y$

A character variable can be compared to another character variable or a literal constant in an IF statement; for example:

      120 IF R$ = "YES" THEN 190

Techniques for defining and using character variables vary significantly among different versions of BASIC. Some versions allocate enough space to hold fifteen or sixteen characters. Others determine the length of the field by counting the number of characters first assigned to the field (by a LET statement or an INPUT statement). Others assign one character unless the programmer explicitly requests more. Check with your instructor for your system's standards.

The First Subroutine: Gross Pay

What does the skeleton mainline tell us? Of what use is it? It defines the order in which computations are to be performed, a critical function in any program. We can test it; by running the skeleton mainline and inputting test data, we can verify that the program does, in fact, produce correct answers. It is time to begin adding functions.

Let's consider the gross pay computation first. How do we compute gross pay? Basically, it is the product of hours worked and an hourly pay rate. There is, however, more to it. We would like to add an overtime pay computation: all hours over 40 are paid at "time and a half".

Logically, what must we do to incorporate this new computation? The first step is to determine if overtime is to be paid. This involves a test: is "hours worked" greater than 40? If it is, gross pay will include overtime; if not, gross pay will be computed using the old rule (Fig. 5.4).

We know the regular pay algorithm; using the variable names of the program, it is:

      G = H * R.

Fig. 5.2: *A flowchart of our skeleton mainline.*

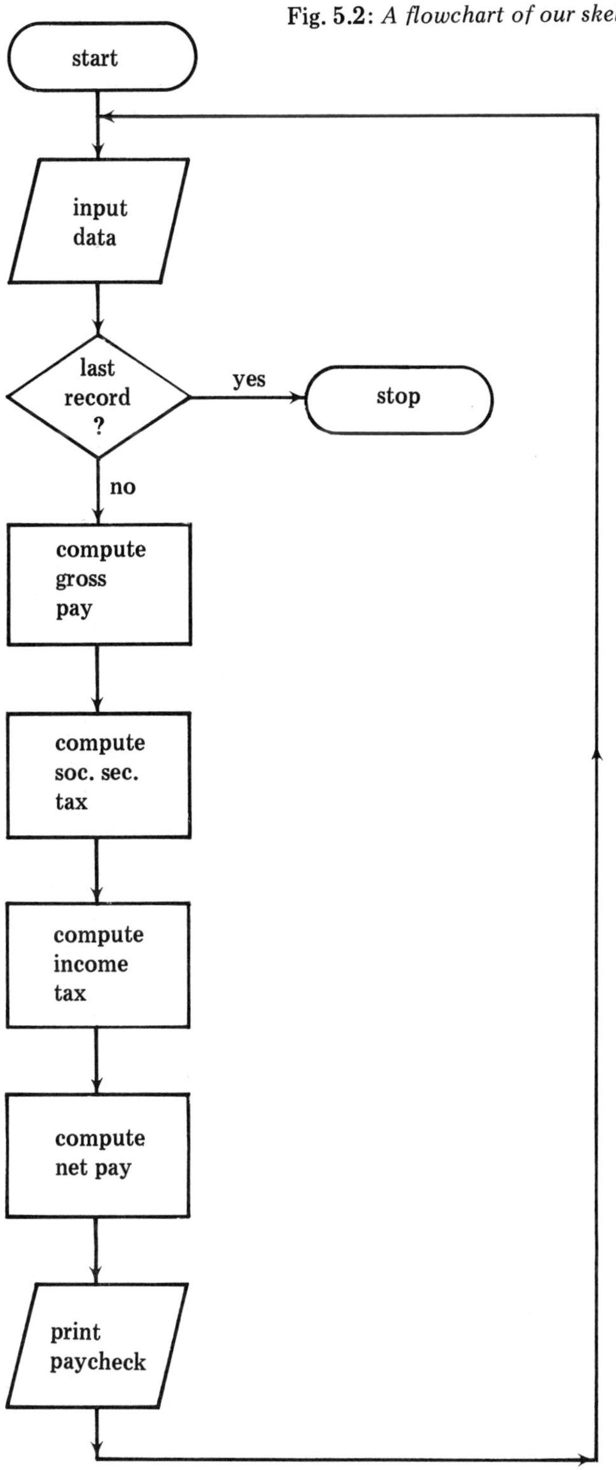

Fig. 5.3: *The skeleton mainline in BASIC.*

```
100 REM * THIS PROGRAM COMPUTES AND PRINTS    *
110 REM * AN INDIVIDUAL'S TAKE-HOME PAY.      *
120 REM *                                     *
130 REM *      WRITTEN BY: W.S. DAVIS         *
140 REM *                  NOV. 1             *
150 REM * * * * * * * * * * * * * * * * * * * *
160 REM
170 REM * THE PROGRAM STARTS BY READING
180 REM * ONE INPUT RECORD CONTAINING:
190 REM *   N$    EMPLOYEE NAME
200 REM *   I$    EMPLOYEE INITIALS
210 REM *   H     HOURS WORKED
220 REM *   R     HOURLY PAY RATE
230 REM * IF HOURS WORKED IS NEGATIVE,
240 REM * THIS IS THE LAST RECORD.

270 REM * COMPUTE GROSS PAY (G) AND
280 REM * SOCIAL SECURITY TAX (S).

310 REM * COMPUTE INCOME TAX (I)

330 REM * COMPUTE NET PAY (N) AND PRINT CHECK;
340 REM * THEN GO BACK AND READ NEXT RECORD.

390 REM * * * * * * * * * * * * * * * * * * * *
400 REM * AT END OF DATA, TERMINATE PROGRAM   *
410 REM * * * * * * * * * * * * * * * * * * * *

250 INPUT N$,I$,H,R
260 IF H<0 THEN 420
290 LET G=H*R
300 LET S=G*.0665
320 LET I=G*.1
350 LET D=S+I
360 LET N=G-D
370 PRINT N$;I$, "$";N
380 GOTO 250
420 END
```

Fig. 5.4: *Gross pay logic.*

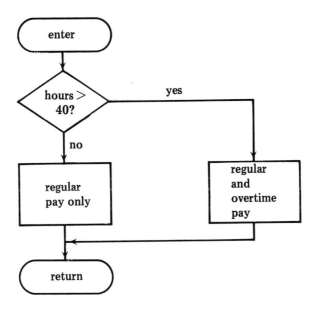

How do we compute overtime? Two computations will be involved. First, regular pay for the first 40 hours can be computed from:

$$G = H * 40$$

The number of hours of overtime is equal to the actual number of hours worked minus 40. These hours are paid at 1½ times the usual rate. Adding this algorithm to the earlier one yields:

$$G = (H * 40) + (H - 40) * (R * 1.5)$$

Do we really need all those parenthesis? No, but they make the algorithm easier to read.

Given these two algorithms, we can now write a subroutine to compute gross pay; it is shown in Fig. 5.5 Assuming that H and R are known, the subroutine will compute gross pay. Now, how can we attach it to the mainline?

GOSUB and RETURN

Subroutines are linked to a mainline through the GOSUB and RETURN statements. Consider, for example, the code outlined in Fig. 5.6. As the mainline instructions are executed, the program will eventually come to instruction number 250. The command is: GOSUB 500. As a result the program branches to instruction number 500, and begins executing the subroutine instructions. The GOSUB, however, is not exactly a branch. Before the transfer to statement number 500, the computer notes that the GOSUB instruction was number 250. Later, we'll see why this "note" is so important.

Fig. 5.5: *A subroutine to compute gross pay.*

```
1000                    REM * * * * * * * * * * * * * * * *
1010                    REM * SUBROUTINE TO COMPUTE GROSS PAY.
1020                    REM * BASE PAY IS THE PRODUCT OF HOURS
1030                    REM * WORKED AND THE HOURLY PAY RATE.
1040                    REM * ALL HOURS OVER 40 ARE PAID AT 1.5
1050                    REM * TIMES THE REGULAR HOURLY RATE.
1060                    REM * * * * * * * * * * * * * * * *
1070 IF H>40 THEN 1100
1080 LET G=H*R
1090 GOTO 1110
1100 LET G=40*R+(H-40)*(R*1.5)
1110 RETURN
```

The subroutine statements are now executing. Eventually, statement number 550, the RETURN statement, is reached. When the computer encounters a RETURN statement, control is transferred back to the statement immediately following the GOSUB, in this case, number 260. How is this transfer achieved? Remember that the system noted the location of the GOSUB. Given this note, it is easy to find the "next" instruction.

Adding the Subroutine to the Mainline

We already have a skeleton mainline. How do we add the new subroutine? In the skeleton program, gross pay is computed through a dummy instruction. We'll simply replace the dummy instruction with a GOSUB (Fig. 5.7), referencing the first executable statement in the subroutine: GOSUB 1070. (Note: remarks are not executed.) Now when we run the program, the input data will be read; then control will be given to the gross pay subroutine, where a detailed computation will be performed. Then it's back to the mainline for other dummy computations before the results are printed.

A few other minor changes are necessary. The END statement must be the last statement in the program, so it must be moved; we have shifted it to statement number 9999, which clearly puts it at the end. We do want our program to terminate when the end of data condition is reached, so we need something to replace the END statement in the skeleton program. In Fig. 5.7, the statement:

420 STOP

Fig. 5.6: *GOSUB and RETURN.*

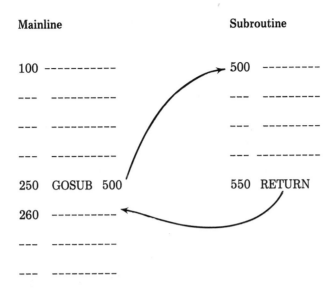

Mainline   Subroutine

100 ----------   ▶ 500 ---------

--- ----------   --- ---------

--- ----------   --- ---------

--- ----------   --- ---------

250 GOSUB 500   550 RETURN

260 ---------- ◀

--- ----------

--- ----------

can be seen. A STOP statement terminates a program. An END statement terminates a program *and* announces that there are (physically) no more statements in the program. Do you see the difference? You can have as many STOP statements as you need in a program, but you may have only one END.

Finally, statement number 990 is simply a REM followed by a row of dashes. This remark serves to visually separate the mainline from the subroutines; it is a documentation aid, nothing more. A second documentation aid was the choice of statement numbers used in the subroutine. Numbers up to 999 were reserved for the mainline. Statement numbers 1000 through 1999 belong to the first subroutine. Later, when a second subroutine is added, numbers 2000 through 2999 will be used. While not essential, such techniques greatly improve a program's readability. If a program is easier to read, it is easier to debug, modify, and maintain, and that is definitely to the programmer's advantage.

As is so often the case, different versions of BASIC do things differently. Not all recognize the STOP statement; if your system doesn't, when you are ready to terminate the program simply branch (GOTO) the END statement. Some systems allow a REM statement to be the target of a GOSUB, GOTO, or IF; most do not. Even if your system does allow such branches, transferring control to a remark or comment is not considered good programming form and should be avoided.

On most systems, the REM statement is treated as a comment. It is not really part of the program, so it doesn't take up main memory space or slow the program down. On other systems, particularly microcomputer systems, this is not the case. Because of the nature of such systems, every statement must be treated in the same way; thus a REM statement occupies memory and is "executed" each time the program is run. Using multiple REM statements can have a very negative impact on such systems, and yet the REM statement is essential to good documentation. How can the microcomputer programmer get around this problem? Frequently, comments are typed, off-line, on a regular typewriter, and simply taped to the finished program listing.

Testing the New Version of the Program

We are now ready to test the new version of our payroll program (Fig. 5.7). We'll run the program and enter our test data, perhaps the same test data used earlier to test the skeleton mainline. To be certain that everything is working properly, some of that data should be for people who worked more than 40 hours, with other data for people who worked less than 40 hours. For those who worked overtime, the answers should be different from those produced by the skeleton program; for those who didn't, the answers should be the same.

What if the answers are wrong? They were correct before the gross pay subroutine was added. What was changed? Only the gross pay subroutine. Where would we expect to find the error? Clearly, in the gross pay subroutine. The fact that modular program design tends to narrow the search for errors to a single module is one of its most significant advantages.

Eventually, the test data will generate the expected answers. The gross pay subroutine will have passed our test. Thus we'll be ready to add another computational routine to the program.

The Second Subroutine: Income Tax

Social security tax is 6.65% of gross pay, and, except for a condition that we will not consider here, the dummy statement is correct. Thus we turn our attention to the computation of income tax.

Our first task, as always, is to define the problem. We want to compute income tax. How do we do it? What are the rules, the algorithms?

The federal government publishes a book (*Circular E: Employer's Tax Guide*) in which the rules are clearly defined. The specific tax tables are just a bit more complex than we need to illustrate the concepts of this chapter, so we'll make up a simplified table that works in much the same way. Assume that the tax table we are to use is defined as follows:

```
100                          REM * THIS PROGRAM COMPUTES AND PRINTS  *
110                          REM * AN INDIVIDUAL'S TAKE-HOME PAY.     *
120                          REM *                                    *
130                          REM *    WRITTEN BY: W.S. DAVIS          *
140                          REM *              NOV. 1                *
150                          REM * * * * * * * * * * * * * * * * * * *
160                          REM
170                          REM * THE PROGRAM STARTS BY READING
180                          REM * ONE INPUT RECORD CONTAINING:
190                          REM *   N$       EMPLOYEE NAME
200                          REM *   I$       EMPLOYEE INITIALS
210                          REM *   H        HOURS WORKED
220                          REM *   R        HOURLY PAY RATE
230                          REM * IF HOURS WORKED IS NEGATIVE,
240                          REM * THIS IS THE LAST RECORD.
250 INPUT N$,I$,H,R
260 IF H<0 THEN 420
270                          REM * COMPUTE GROSS PAY (G) AND
280                          REM * SOCIAL SECURITY TAX (S).
290 GOSUB 1070
300 LET S=G*.0665
310                          REM * COMPUTE INCOME TAX (I)
320 LET I=G*.1
330                          REM * COMPUTE NET PAY (N) AND PRINT CHECK;
340                          REM * THEN GO BACK AND READ NEXT RECORD.
350 LET D=S+I
360 LET N=G-D
370 PRINT N$;I$,"$";N
380 GOTO 250
390                          REM * * * * * * * * * * * * * * * * * * *
400                          REM * AT END OF DATA, TERMINATE PROGRAM *
410                          REM * * * * * * * * * * * * * * * * * * *
420 STOP
990 REM -------------------------------------------------------------
1000                         REM * * * * * * * * * * * * * * * * *
1010                         REM * SUBROUTINE TO COMPUTE GROSS PAY.
1020                         REM * BASE PAY IS THE PRODUCT OF HOURS
1030                         REM * WORKED AND THE HOURLY PAY RATE.
1040                         REM * ALL HOURS OVER 40 ARE PAID AT 1.5
1050                         REM * TIMES THE REGULAR HOURLY RATE.
1060                         REM * * * * * * * * * * * * * * * * *
1070 IF H>40 THEN 1100
1080 LET G=H*R
1090 GOTO 1110
1100 LET G=40*R+(H-40)*(R*1.5)
1110 RETURN
9999 END
```

If gross pay is:	tax is
$0 – $100	10% of gross
$100 – $200	$10 + 20% of gross earnings over $100
$200 and up	$30 + 30% of gross earnings over $200

What if an employee earned $150? For gross pay between $100 and $200, the tax is $10 plus 20 percent of the amount of gross earnings over $100. This excess amount (150 – 100) is $50. Twenty percent of $50 is $10. The tax due is, therefore, $20. Suppose another employee earns $400 in gross pay. This person falls into the highest bracket, paying $30 plus a percentage. The percentage tax would be 30 percent of (400 – 200), which is $60. The base tax is $30. The total tax due is $90.

Now that we understand the income tax algorithm (and the best way to gain such an understanding is to do a few test computations), we can begin to consider the BASIC code needed to compute the amount of tax due. The fact that we understand the algorithm does not, however, mean that we know how to code it. Additional planning is necessary.

Logically, how would you use the table to compute tax? The key, of course, is gross pay. Using gross pay, the proper tax bracket can be found, and the tax computed.

The first step might be to compare gross pay with 100, the upper limit of the first bracket. If gross is greater than 100, this employee falls into a higher bracket; if not, we have located the correct bracket and can compute the tax. For those whose gross pay was greater than 100, a comparison against 200, the limit of the second bracket, can be made. Once again, the result of this test can be used to determine if the program will compute the tax using the factors of the second bracket, or move on to the third. This logic is flowcharted in Fig. 5.8.

Now we can write the subroutine (Fig. 5.9). Note that the subroutine assumes that G (for gross pay) is known. Where does G come from? The main program must provide this value. Note also that we have used statement numbers 2000 through 2170; the 2000's have been reserved for this subroutine, making it easier to distinguish it from the other subroutines. Fig. 5.10 shows the payroll program with the income tax subroutine in place.

Once again, it is time to test the program. The test data should generate gross pay values in each tax bracket; only if each component of a program is tested can we be confident of its accuracy. What if some of the answers are wrong? They were correct before; we added just one function; thus, the error must lie in this new subroutine. As soon as the income tax subroutine has been successfully debugged, we'll be ready to add yet another subroutine.

Fig. 5.8: *Testing to find the proper tax bracket.*

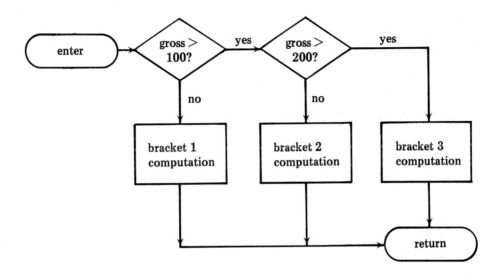

Fig. 5.9: *The income tax subroutine.*

```
2000          REM * * * * * * * * * * * * * * * * * *
2010          REM * SUBROUTINE TO COMPUTE INCOME TAX.
2020          REM * THE TAX RATE CAN BE FOUND BY USING
2030          REM * THE COMPUTED GROSS PAY TO SEARCH
2040          REM * THE FOLLOWING TABLE:
2050          REM *     GROSS      TAX
2060          REM *      0-100     10% OF GROSS
2070          REM *    100-200     $10 + 20% OF G - 100
2080          REM *    200 AND UP  $30 + 30% OF G - 200
2090          REM * * * * * * * * * * * * * * * * * *
2100 IF G>100 THEN 2130
2110 LET I=G*.1
2120 GOTO 2170
2130 IF G>200 THEN 2160
2140 LET I=10+(G-100)*.2
2150 GOTO 2170
2160 LET I=30+(G-200)*.3
2170 RETURN
```

MODULAR PROGRAM DESIGN

What next? More subroutines can be added. One might take care of the input operation, reading some data, checking the values for reasonability, and making certain that only "good" data are passed to the rest of the program. Routines for state income tax and local income tax might be added. Other subroutines would incorporate other deductions. Additional gross pay complexities can be woven in. The program is likely to be very large and very complex by the time we finish, but, given the step by step approach to design and implementation, it should work. Do you begin to see the value of the modular approach to program design?

The philosophy is simple: take a complex problem, break it into simple problems, and solve each one separately; then put the partial solutions together. If you remember this simple rule, programming is easy. Think first. Then do it.

SUMMARY

The chapter began by discussing the complexity frequently found in real world programming problems. When faced with a complex problem, the programmer will often break it into smaller pieces and then attack the pieces one at a time. This is the essence of a modular approach to program design.

The problem described in the chapter was a payroll program. A hierarchy chart of the program was developed, identifying the major computational modules. Then a skeleton mainline was written and tested. The idea of character variables (defined in BASIC by a letter followed by a dollar sign) was introduced.

We then turned our attention to the computational subroutines, writing the logic needed to implement a somewhat more complex gross pay routine and an income tax routine. The subroutines were linked to the mainline by using GOSUB and RETURN statements. The chapter closed with a few comments on the value of the modular approach to program design.

EXERCISES

1.   Assume that a new union contract calls for a shift premium of 10% to be added to the gross pay of all employees working the second shift. According to the contract, gross pay is to be computed as before, and then, if the employee works second shift, this 10% premium is to be added. How would you modify the chapter program to include this new feature? Would you have to add anything to the INPUT statement? Make the necessary changes and run the program.

2.   Assume that the people working for our firm live in three different areas, city A, city B, and city C. Each city has a local income tax, charging the following rates:

Fig. 5.10: *The payroll program with the income tax subroutine in place.*

```
100                           REM * THIS PROGRAM COMPUTES AND PRINTS  *
110                           REM * AN INDIVIDUAL'S TAKE-HOME PAY.     *
120                           REM *                                    *
130                           REM *    WRITTEN BY: W.S. DAVIS          *
140                           REM *              NOV. 1                *
150                           REM * * * * * * * * * * * * * * * * * * *
160                           REM
170                           REM * THE PROGRAM STARTS BY READING
180                           REM * ONE INPUT RECORD CONTAINING:
190                           REM *    N$       EMPLOYEE NAME
200                           REM *    I$       EMPLOYEE INITIALS
210                           REM *    H        HOURS WORKED
220                           REM *    R        HOURLY PAY RATE
230                           REM * IF HOURS WORKED IS NEGATIVE,
240                           REM * THIS IS THE LAST RECORD.
250 INPUT N$,I$,H,R
260 IF H<0 THEN 420
270                           REM * COMPUTE GROSS PAY (G) AND
280                           REM * SOCIAL SECURITY TAX (S).
290 GOSUB 1070
300 LET S=G*.0665
310                           REM * COMPUTE INCOME TAX (I)
320 GOSUB 2100
330                           REM * COMPUTE NET PAY (N) AND PRINT CHECK;
340                           REM * THEN GO BACK AND READ NEXT RECORD.
350 LET D=S+I
360 LET N=G-D
370 PRINT N$;I$,"$";N
380 GOTO 250
390                           REM * * * * * * * * * * * * * * * * * * *
400                           REM * AT END OF DATA, TERMINATE PROGRAM *
410                           REM * * * * * * * * * * * * * * * * * * *
420 STOP
990 REM -----------------------------------------------------------
1000                          REM * * * * * * * * * * * * * * * * * * *
1010                          REM * SUBROUTINE TO COMPUTE GROSS PAY.
1020                          REM * BASE PAY IS THE PRODUCT OF HOURS
1030                          REM * WORKED AND THE HOURLY PAY RATE.
1040                          REM * ALL HOURS OVER 40 ARE PAID AT 1.5
1050                          REM * TIMES THE REGULAR HOURLY RATE.
1060                          REM * * * * * * * * * * * * * * * * * * *
1070 IF H>40 THEN 1100
1080 LET G=H*R
1090 GOTO 1110
1100 LET G=40*R+(H-40)*(R*1.5)
1110 RETURN
2000                          REM * * * * * * * * * * * * * * * * * * *
2010                          REM * SUBROUTINE TO COMPUTE INCOME TAX.
2020                          REM * THE TAX RATE CAN BE FOUND BY USING
2030                          REM * THE COMPUTED GROSS PAY TO SEARCH
2040                          REM * THE FOLLOWING TABLE:
2050                          REM *      GROSS       TAX
2060                          REM *      0-100       10% OF GROSS
2070                          REM *      100-200     $10 + 20% OF G - 100
2080                          REM *      200 AND UP  $30 + 30% OF G - 200
2090                          REM * * * * * * * * * * * * * * * * * * *
2100 IF G>100 THEN 2130
2110 LET I=G*.1
2120 GOTO 2170
2130 IF G>200 THEN 2160
2140 LET I=10+(G-100)*.2
2150 GOTO 2170
2160 LET I=30+(G-200)*.3
2170 RETURN
9999 END
```

City	Rate
A	1.0%
B	0.5%
C	1.5%

Add a subroutine (and necessary linkage) to the payroll program to compute local income tax; don't forget to consider this deduction in computing net pay. Once again, you may have to add something to input. What?

3. Many states have a state income tax. If your state does, get a tax withholding table (try your school's payroll department) and add a subroutine to the payroll program to compute this tax.

4. Add a subroutine to compute union dues. The rule is: if gross pay is less than $150, dues are $2.50; otherwise, dues are $5.00.

5. Modify the income tax subroutine of the chapter payroll program to consider the following factor. Tax should not be computed based on the amount of gross pay. Instead, the basis for entering the table should be taxable income, which is computed by subtracting from gross pay $7.50 for each dependent (child, spouse, etc.) claimed. What changes must be made to input? Be careful in your computations; it is possible to have a negative taxable income.

6. Write a program to compute and print performance statistics for a baseball team. Input data will be as follows:

Hitters	Pitchers
number	number
name	name
times at bat	innings pitched
hits	earned runs
H, for hitter	P, for pitcher

Your program should read the input record and determine the player's position from the code (H for hitter, P for pitcher). For all hitters, link to a subroutine and compute the batting average, which is defined as:

$$AVERAGE = HITS / AT BATS$$

For all pitchers, compute the earned run average, which is defined as:

$$ERA = RUNS / (INNINGS/9);$$

once again, use a subroutine. Following computations, print the player's number, name, and other relevant data.

7. Chapter 3, problem 5 asked you to write a program to compute the factorial of an integer. Chapter 4, problem 16 used factorials in computing (or estimating) a sine. Redo the latter problem, writing a subroutine to compute a factorial.

8. In statistics and probability, it is often necessary to compute the number of different possible outcomes of an event. By computing the number of combinations or permutations, it is sometimes possible to find this number of different possible outcomes. For "n" things taken "r" at a time, the formula for combinations is:

$$\frac{n!}{r!\,(n-r)!}$$

and the formula for permutations is

$$\frac{n!}{(n-r)!}$$

where n! is "n factorial".

Write a program to read a value for n and a value for r and compute the number of combinations and permutations possible. Note that r must be less than n. Since several factorials must be computed, it is strongly recommended that you code the factorial routine as a subroutine.

9. Write a program to generate electric bills. Input to the program will consist of a rate code, a user number, and the number of kilowatt hours used. Develop a skeleton mainline first. The rate charged for electricity is based on the rate code. In the skeleton mainline, use the following simplified rate table:

Code	Meaning	Rate
1	Regular household	2½ cents/kilowatt hour
2	Total electricity	2 cents/kilowatt hour
3	Factory	1½ cents/kilowatt hour
4	Non-profit	1 cent/kilowatt hour

The skeleton mainline should read an input record, determine the proper rate by checking the rate code, compute the bill from the skeleton formula, and print the customer number, the number of kilowatt hours used, and the amount of the bill. Be sure to include test data for each of the four rates.

10. Modify the program of exercise 9, adding a subroutine to compute the actual electric bill for a regular household (rate code = 1), using the folowing table:

Base charge	$3.00
First 1000 kilowatt hrs	2.49 cents per kilowatt hour
Additional kilowatt hrs	1.60 cents per kilowatt hour
Fuel adjustment	1.6399 cents per kilowatt hour

Note that the base charge is added to the bill no matter how many kilowatt hours are used; in other words, even if the usage is zero, the charge is a minimum of $3.00. If usage is greater than zero, the charge is $3.00 plus the charge per kilowatt hour. The fuel adjustment is an extra charge added to *all* kilowatt hours used.

11. Add subroutines for other rate codes, using the following rules:

Code	Base Charge	Charge/kilowatt after				Fuel
		0	1000	2000	5000	Adj.
2	$ 3.00	2.49 cents	1.60 cents	1.25 cents	1.25 cents	1.6399 cents
3	$50.00	0	0	1.00 cents	0.75 cents	1.6399 cents
4	$ 5.00	1.25 cents	1.25 cents	0.75 cents	0.75 cents	1.6399 cents

12. Loan officers in a bank often find it necessary to do interest computations. Among the questions they must answer are:

a. If I invest P dollars today, at i% interest, how much will I have after n years? The formula is:

$$F = P(1+i)^n$$

b. I want to have F dollars n years from now. How much must I invest today at i% interest? The formula is:

$$F = F/(1+i)^n$$

c. If I deposit R dollars each year for n years, how much will I have (at i% interest)? The formula is:

$$F = R \; \frac{(1+i)^{n} - 1}{i}$$

d. I need F dollars in n years. How much must I invest each year at i% interest? The formula is:

$$R = F \; \frac{i}{(1+i)^{n} - 1}$$

e. If I borrow P dollars today for n years, how much must I repay each year at i% interest? The formula is:

$$R = P \; \frac{i(1+i)^{n}}{(1+i)^{n} - 1}$$

f. How much is a promise to pay R dollars per year for n years at i% interest worth today? The formula is:

$$P = R \; \frac{(1+i)^{n} - 1}{i(1+i)^{n}}$$

Write a program to input a code identifying the interest computation to be performed (A, B, C, D, E, or F). Then input a dollar amount (either P, F, or R depending on the computation to be performed), the interest rate, and the number of years. The six interest computation formulas should be located in six computational subroutines; link to the proper subroutine and do the computations. Then print the input values and the computed answer. Don't forget to clearly identify your results.

13. Simulation is a most interesting application of the computer. As an elementary simulation exercise, write a program to simulate the rolling of a pair of dice.

The secret to simulating is the use of random numbers. The BASIC function RND is used to generate a random number between 0 and 1. It is coded as either:

```
110  LET  Y = RND(X)
```

or as:

```
110  LET  Y = RND
```

depending on the version of BASIC used. A single die has six surfaces numbered 1 through 6, we can simulate the result of rolling that die. Since RND returns a value between 0 and 1, we can get 1, 2, 3, 4, 5, or 6 by coding:

130 LET V = INT(RND * 6 + 1)

Multiplying the value returned by RND by 6 yields a value between 0 and 6; in other words, the value is greater than 0 but less than 6. Adding 1 gives us a number greater than 1 but less than 7. Taking the integer portion of this number (the INT function) drops the fractional portion leaving only the whole number—the result will be 1, 2, 3, 4, 5, or 6.

Your program should begin by generating two rolls of a single die. Print the two values and their sum. Then ask the player if he or she wishes to continue—use the response to control the loop. Place the routine that generates random numbers between 1 and 6 in a subroutine.

Once you have written this skeleton program, you may want to add some "bells and whistles" of your own. Consider, for example, the logic needed to allow a single player to bet against the computer. Consider dice games involving multiple players. Consider implementing the rules of craps. As you extend your program, don't forget to use subroutines for introducing new functions.

14.   There are 52 cards in a deck. Assign the number 1 through 4 to the aces, 5 through 8 to the kings, and so on. Generate random numbers between 1 and 52; simply multiply RND by 52, add 1, and take the integer portion. Write a program to play a game of acey/duecy or high/low. Use your random number function to select two cards. The player then bets. If the next card lies between the first two, the player wins; if not, the computer wins. Use subroutines for the random number function and to figure out the value of the card. You might also consider using a subroutine to keep track of the player's winnings and losings.

6

Arrays
and Data Statements

OVERVIEW

In a typical program, data is input, processed, and then the results are output. A second cycle of the program involves a different set of data. Each data element is used once, and does not impact subsequent repetitions of the program.

Occasionally, the programmer will encounter a problem where the same data is needed more than once. The option of retyping is always available, of course, but retyping is time-consuming and error prone. It is much better to enter the data once and store it in the computer. Once the data has been stored, it can be used as often as is necessary.

In this chapter, we will consider such a problem. Initially, an array will be used to hold the data. Later, we will consider the use of READ/DATA statements.

STANDARDIZED TEST SCORING

Is there any student in the United States who has never taken a standardized test? Probably not. With IQ tests, interest tests, achievement tests, and college entrance examinations, most students have been exposed to several.

The scores earned on such tests are a bit unusual. An IQ test uses 100 as the average. College board scores range from a low of 200 to a high of 800; on the ACT test, scores range from 0 to 30. What is a "passing" score? There isn't any! In fact, that is the point. Standardized tests are not designed to generate grades on an A, B, C scale. Instead, they are designed to rank a student with respect to others who took the same test. It is this relative ranking that is important, and not some arbitrary grading scheme. Designers of standardized tests go out of their way to report scores that are difficult to convert to traditional grades.

Imagine that we have been assigned the task of writing a program to compute and print the scores on such an exam. We will use as our model the SAT (Scholastic Aptitute Test). Each student's score is to fall between 200 and 800, with an average of 500. How might we go about developing such a program?

DESIGNING THE ALGORITHM

The first step is to very clearly define the algorithm or algorithms involved in computing a score. It's one thing to state that scores should lie between 200 and 800, with an average of 500. It is quite different to define *precisely* how such scores are to be computed.

Each student who takes the exam earns a *raw score*, the number of questions answered correctly. Often, to adjust for random guessing, a factor based on the number of questions answered incorrectly is used, but the raw score essentially measures a student's correct answers.

The key to converting raw scores into relative scores on a 200-800 scale is the *average raw score*; add the raw scores of all the students, divide by the number of students, and you have the average. If your score is *exactly* equal to the average, you should earn a 500; if you did better than average, you should earn more than 500; if you did worse, your examination score will be below 500. The rule we will use (which may not be exactly the same as that used by the people at Educational Testing Service) is:

$$\text{Exam score} = \frac{\text{student raw score}}{\text{average raw score}} * 500$$

An average raw score will generate an exam score of 500. An above average raw score yields an exam score greater than 500. If the raw score is below average, the ratio (student raw/average raw) must be less than 1, so the computed score must be less than 500.

Consider, for example, the following three students:

Student	Raw Score	Raw/Average	Exam Score
Aaron	150	1.5	750
Baker	100	1.0	500
Cooper	50	0.5	250

The raw scores are, respectively, 150, 100, and 50. The average raw score (sum the three and divide by 3) is 100. Aaron's ratio is thus 150/100, which is 1.5; Baker's ratio is 100/100, which is 1.0; Cooper's is 50/100, which is 0.5. Multiplying each ratio by 500 generates the scores shown in the rightmost column.

How can we make certain that all the scores lie between 200 and 800? If the computed examination score is greater than 800, it is made equal to 800, and if the score is less than 200, it is made equal to 200. That, basically, completes the algorithm.

THE PROBLEM: THE DATA MUST BE USED TWICE

There is only one problem with this algorithm: the input data must be used *twice*. How is the average raw score computed? Each input raw score must be read, counted, and accumulated. How are the individual examination scores computed? Each raw score must be compared with the average raw score. Obviously, the average raw score must be known before any of the individual examination scores can be computed. *All* the data must be used to find the average, and then *all* the data must be used *again* to compute individual scores.

It is possible, of course, to input the data twice. As long as there is only a tiny amount of data, this might be reasonable, but if a significant amount of data must be entered, inputting it twice would be both time-consuming and error prone. There must be a better way. There must be a way to enter the data once, store it within the computer, and then use it again as necessary. Actually, there are several ways. In this chapter, we'll be exploring two: arrays and READ/DATA statements.

ARRAYS

Let's consider arrays first. Assume that we will be reading a total of 25 raw scores. How can we store all these scores in the computer? One alternative might be to define 25 different variables: R0 through R9, S0 through S9, and T1 through T5, for example. We could then:

        100   INPUT R0, R1, R2, . . . and so on.

Later, we could sum these values by coding:

        130   LET A = R0 + R1 + R2 + . . ., and so on,

until all the values were added. Finally, each variable could be divided by the computed average raw score to get the final examination scores.

Imagine keeping track of all those variables. Now imagine the same problem with 50 scores. 100! Ridiculous. Once again, there must be a better way. Twenty-five values require twenty-five storage locations. If each value is to be used independently (and it must be), then each storage location must have a unique name. However, the twenty-five raw scores are not really all that different; they are different values of the *same* statistic. They are related. Often, the best way to handle such data is to define an array.

Defining an Array

An array is simply a series of consecutive memory locations. It is defined by coding a **DIM** (for DIMension) statement. Consider, for example, the comparison sketched in Fig. 6.1. On the left is the space assigned to the variable X; it consists of a single memory location (on most systems, a single *word*). On the right is the space assigned to the array defined by:

10 DIM Y(4)

It consists of four consecutive memory locations. (The number in parenthesis defines the number of elements in the array.)

How do we differentiate between these four memory locations? We use subscripts. The first location in the array is Y(1), or Y-sub-1. The second element is Y(2), the third is Y(3), and so on. The subscript is nothing more than the number of the element in the array.

Using an Array

An array element can be used just like any regular variable. For example, the statement:

80 LET Y(1) = 15

would initialize the first element in the array to the value 15, while:

90 LET Y(2) = 0

would set the second element to zero.

We can also use subscripted variables in an INPUT statement. The statement:

80 INPUT Y(1), Y(2), Y(3), Y(4)

might be used to allow the programmer to provide through a terminal initial values for each of the array elements.

Fig. 6.1: *A comparison between the memory space set aside to hold a regular variable and the space needed to hold an array.*

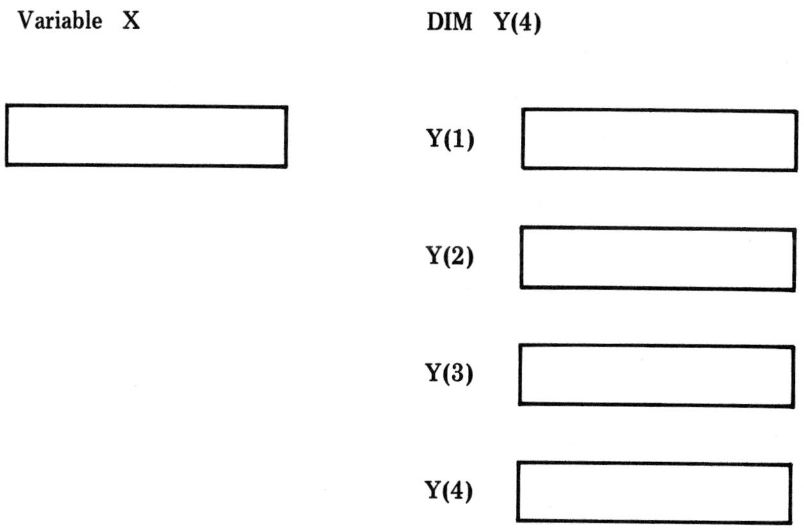

Variable X   DIM Y(4)

Y(1)

Y(2)

Y(3)

Y(4)

The subscript need not, however, be a constant; we can use a variable instead. Consider, for example, the following loop:

```
100  FOR  N = 1  TO  4

110       INPUT  Y(N)

120  NEXT  N
```

Assuming that an array named Y had been created by an earlier DIM statement, this loop could be used to initialize the array. In Fig. 6.2, the process of filling the array is illustrated step by step. As the loop begins, N is set equal to 1 (Fig. 6.2a). The INPUT statement is executed, a prompt is printed on the terminal, and the programmer responds. As the first number comes into the computer, N is equal to 1. Thus Y(N) is really Y(1). The value is stored at memory location Y(1).

Fig. 6.2: *Filling an array (a).*

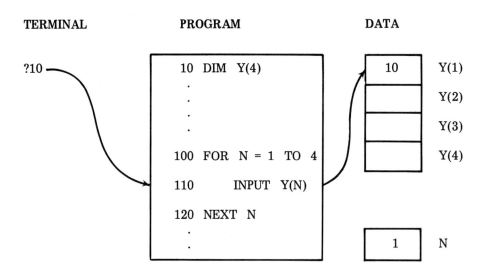

The second time through the loop (Fig. 6.2b), the value of N will be 2. Once again the INPUT statement will be executed; once again a prompt will be displayed; once again the programmer will respond with a value. As this second value goes into the computer, N is 2. Thus Y(N) really means Y(2). The second value is stored at memory location Y(2).

The third time through, N will be 3. Thus the value will be stored at location Y(3)—see Fig. 6.2c. This process continues (Fig. 6.2d) until the loop ends.

Can the elements in an array be used in a LET statement? Yes. Consider, for example, the loop:

        200 FOR K = 1 TO 4

        210   LET A = A + Y(N)

        220 NEXT N

This loop would accumulate all the elements of the array.

Fig. 6.2: *Filling an array (b).*

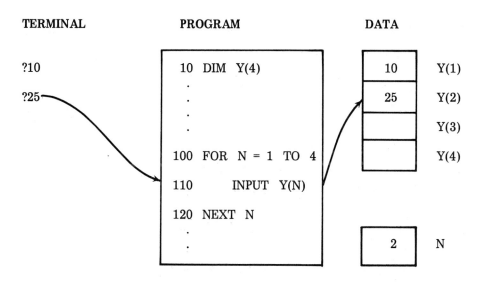

Fig. 6.2: *Filling an array (c).*

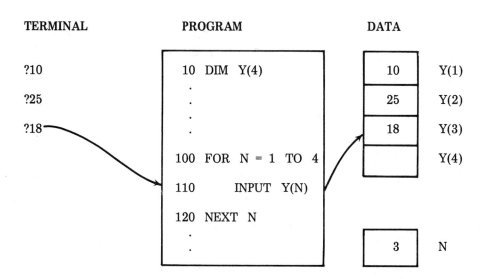

Fig. 6.2: *Filling an array (d).*

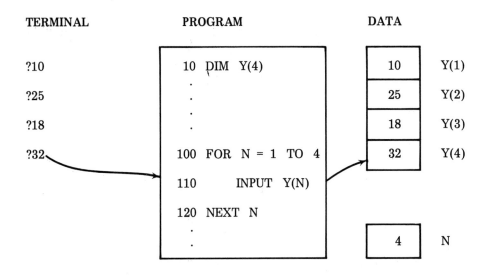

USING AN ARRAY IN THE EXAMINATION SCORING PROBLEM

Earlier in the chapter, we developed an algorithm for an examination scoring problem. The input data was needed twice: once to compute the average raw score, and again to compute the individual examination scores. Using an array is an excellent way to handle this problem. Initially, the data can be read into an array. Once in, the array elements can be summed as part of the "average computation" logic. Later, the same array elements can be used to compute the individual scores.

How would we structure such a program? A number of steps are involved. The problem can become quite lengthy and thus quite complex. As was the case in Chapter 5, when we are faced with a potentially complex problem, the best strategy is often to break it into relatively simple modules. We can identify three such modules in this program; they are (Fig. 6.3):

1. fill the array,

2. compute the average raw score,

3. compute and print the individual exam scores.

Clearly, we must have the data before we can compute the average, and we must have the average before we can compute the examination scores; thus our modular view of the program defines sequence.

Fig. **6.3**: *The structure of the examination scoring program.*

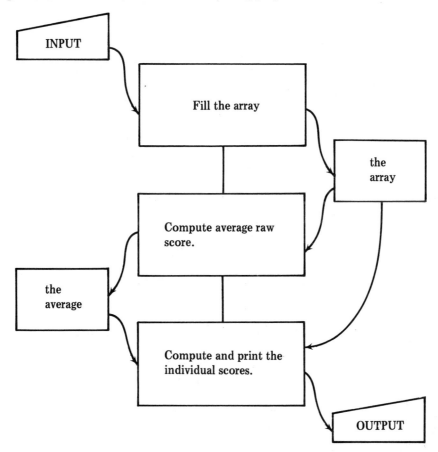

What is it that ties these three basic modules together? The data. Module 1 fills the array; modules 2 and 3 use the data in the array. Module 2 computes the average; module 3 uses the computed average. Except for these data elements, the three modules are independent, so we can code them independently, and put the pieces together later. We must, however, first agree on the data names. We'll define an array named R (for Raw scores), using the following statement:

80 DIM R(25)

The computed average will be called M (for "mean"). We can now begin planning and writing the program logic.

The "Table Fill" Module

The first module fills the table. The logic is simple (Fig. 6.4): input a series of values within a loop, and assign each to the "next" array element. The BASIC code is, in this case, simpler than the flowchart (Fig. 6.5); all we need is a FOR. . .NEXT loop containing an INPUT statement. We'll assume that there are exactly 25 raw scores to be entered.

Fig. 6.4: *The "table fill" logic.*

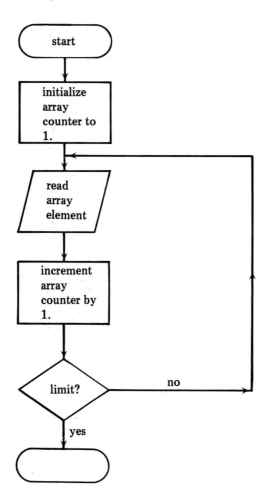

Fig. 6.5: *BASIC code for the "table fill" logic.*

```
 10                    REM * PROGRAM TO COMPUTE SAT SCORES FOR A
 20                    REM * NUMBER OF STUDENTS
 30                    REM *    WRITTEN BY: W.S.DAVIS
 40                    REM *            1/10/81
 50                    REM * * * * * * * * * * * * * * * * * * *
 60                    REM * THE FIRST STEP IS TO FILL A TABLE
 70                    REM * WITH STUDENT RAW SCORES.
 80 DIM R[25]
 90 FOR N=1 TO 25
100    INPUT R[N]
110 NEXT N
```

Fig. 6.6: *The logic of the "compute average" module.*

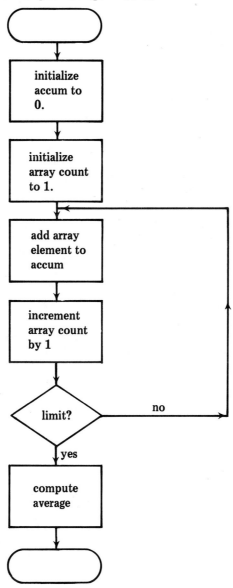

Fig. 6.7: *The BASIC code for the "compute average" module.*

```
120                 REM * NOW, WE COMPUTE THE AVERAGE RAW SCORE
130 LET A=0
140 FOR N=1 TO 25
150    LET A=A+R[N]
160 NEXT N
170 LET M=A/25
```

The "Compute Average" Module

The table is now full, and we can move on to the next bit of logic. How do we compute an average? All the elements in the table must be summed, and this sum must be divided by the number of elements, in this case, 25. The logic is outlined in Fig. 6.6, the code is shown in Fig. 6.7.

The "Compute and Print" Module

Once the average raw score has been computed, we can enter the last phase of the program and compute and print the individual examination scores. Following the printing of a set of headers and the initialization of an array counter to 1, we enter the loop and compute a student's score. Next, we must test to make certain that the limits of 800 and 200 are met. Finally, the computed score can be printed, the array counter (really, the subscript) incremented by 1, and the loop repeated until all the computations have been completed. .

Examination scores are to be printed as whole numbers, with no fractional part. BASIC numbers usually have a fractional part. Thus, the INT function is used on the computed score (Fig. 6.9, statement number 370). You should have little trouble following the logic.

The Complete Program

The time has come to put the pieces together and form a complete program (Fig. 6.10). The program is relatively long and fairly complex. Had we attacked it as a single, large program, we might have encountered difficulty. We decided, however, to break it into pieces. Instead of writing one large program, we wrote three small ones. A potentially difficult task was greatly simplified.

Is there room for improvement? Of course! For example, it might be possible to combine the loop that reads values and fills the table, with the loop that accumulates the values, thus saving several steps. It would certainly be desirable to generalize this program so that it does not assume *exactly* 25 input values. By adding a counter to the first loop, exiting the first loop when a critical condition (such as a negative raw score) was encountered, and then using the count as the upper limit on subsequent loops, the program would be capable of dealing with any number of raw scores (up to the limit imposed by the size of the array). The time for such attention to detail is now, *after* the logic has been carefully defined. Efficient code is irrelevant if the answers are wrong.

TESTING THE PROGRAM: READ/DATA STATEMENTS

The time has come to test the program. Twenty-five values must be entered; output is displayed only after all twenty-five raw scores have been typed. What if the answers are wrong? Incorrect answers mean that there is a bug in the program. Correct the error and run the program again, typing in twenty-five more values. Continue testing until the results are satisfactory.

Fig. 6.8: *Logic for the "compute and print" module.*

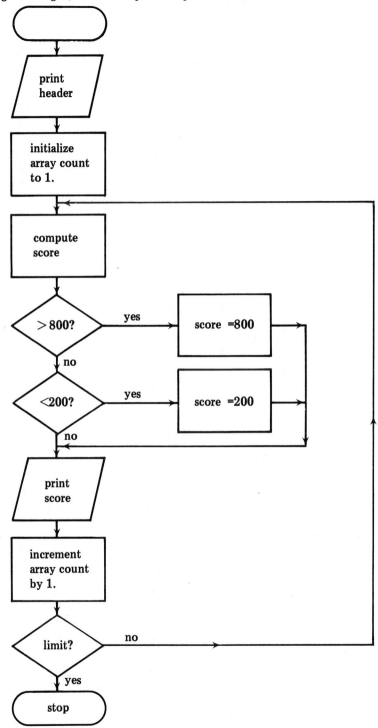

Fig. 6.9: *The BASIC code for the "compute and print" module.*

```
180                   REM * GIVEN THE RAW SCORES AND THE COMPUTED
190                   REM * AVERAGE RAW SCORE, THE STUDENT'S SAT
200                   REM * CAN BE COMPUTED FROM THE FORMULA
210                   REM *    SAT = (RAW / AVG RAW) * 500
220                   REM * USING THIS FORMULA,THE AVERAGE SCORE
230                   REM * WILL BE 500. ADDITIONAL TESTS WILL BE
240                   REM * USED TO ENSURE THAT THE MAXIMUM SAT
250                   REM * SCORE WILL BE 800,AND THE MINIMUM
260                   REM * WILL BE 200. THE FINAL SCORE WILL BE
270                   REM * SHOWN TO ITS NEAREST INTEGER VALUE.
280                   REM *
290 PRINT TAB(10),"STUDENT";TAB(20),"RAW SCORE";TAB(30),"SAT SCORE"
300 FOR N=1 TO 25
310    LET S=(R[N]/M)*500
320    IF S<=800 THEN 350
330    LET S=800
340    GOTO 370
350    IF S>=200 THEN 370
360    LET S=200
370    LET S=INT(S)
380    PRINT TAB(13),N;TAB(23),R[N];TAB(33),S
390 NEXT N
400 END
```

As you may have already discovered, the testing stage may involve several runs. Typing twenty-five values each time can be annoying, as errors are usually obvious after the first few lines of output. One solution is to modify the upper limit on all the loops so that a test can be conducted with fewer values. This is not always a good idea, since the program you will be testing is not really *the* program, and new errors can easily be introduced during the process of changing back.

A better option involves using READ/DATA statements. A **READ** statement is much like an INPUT statement:

```
statement no.    READ    var1, var2, var3, . . .
```

Fig. 6.10: *The complete examination scoring program.*

```
10                        REM * PROGRAM TO COMPUTE SAT SCORES FOR A
20                        REM * NUMBER OF STUDENTS
30                        REM *    WRITTEN BY: W.S.DAVIS
40                        REM *            1/10/81
50                        REM * * * * * * * * * * * * * * * * *
60                        REM * THE FIRST STEP IS TO FILL A TABLE
70                        REM * WITH STUDENT RAW SCORES.
80  DIM R[25]
90  FOR N=1 TO 25
100    INPUT R[N]
110 NEXT N
120                       REM * NOW, WE COMPUTE THE AVERAGE RAW SCORE
130 LET A=0
140 FOR N=1 TO 25
150    LET A=A+R[N]
160 NEXT N
170 LET M=A/25
180                       REM * GIVEN THE RAW SCORES AND THE COMPUTED
190                       REM * AVERAGE RAW SCORE, THE STUDENT'S SAT
200                       REM * CAN BE COMPUTED FROM THE FORMULA
210                       REM *    SAT = (RAW / AVG RAW) * 500
220                       REM * USING THIS FORMULA,THE AVERAGE SCORE
230                       REM * WILL BE 500. ADDITIONAL TESTS WILL BE
240                       REM * USED TO ENSURE THAT THE MAXIMUM SAT
250                       REM * SCORE WILL BE 800,AND THE MINIMUM
260                       REM * WILL BE 200. THE FINAL SCORE WILL BE
270                       REM * SHOWN TO ITS NEAREST INTEGER VALUE.
280                       REM *
290 PRINT TAB(10),"STUDENT";TAB(20),"RAW SCORE";TAB(30),"SAT SCORE"
300 FOR N=1 TO 25
310    LET S=(R[N]/M)*500
320    IF S<=800 THEN 350
330    LET S=800
340    GOTO 370
350    IF S>=200 THEN 370
360    LET S=200
370    LET S=INT(S)
380    PRINT TAB(13),N;TAB(23),R[N];TAB(33),S
390 NEXT N
400 END
```

The statement number is followed by the word READ which is, in turn, followed by a list of variables separated by commas. In revising the examination scoring program, we can simply replace the INPUT statement (number 100 in Fig. 6.10) with:

    100 READ R(N)

Although the READ and INPUT statements look similar and function in much the same way, they are different. An INPUT statement represents a request for the programmer to enter a value through the terminal *after* the program has started to run. A READ statement gets a value from a list of constants that are part of the program. The programmer must supply this list of constants *before* the program is run, by including one or more DATA statements in the program.

A DATA statement consists of the key word DATA followed by a list of constants separated by commas:

> statement no.   DATA   constant-1,constant-2, . . .

The constants can be either numeric or alphanumeric. Any non-numeric constant must be enclosed in a set of quote marks. Fig. 6.11 shows the examination scoring program with READ/DATA statements replacing the INPUT.

How does the READ/DATA combination work? Consider the following example. Given the instructions:

    100 READ X

    110 DATA 10,15,25

the first time the READ instruction is executed, the value 10 (the first constant) will be assigned to variable X. The second time the READ is executed, the second constant, 15, is assigned to X; the third time, 25 is assigned to X. The constants are simply used in sequence. If more than one variable follows the READ, the constants are still used in sequence. For example, given the code:

    250 READ A$,R

    260 DATA "SMITH",200,"JONES",452

the first time the READ is executed, A$ (a character variable) will be assigned the value "SMITH", and R will be assigned the value 200. The second time the READ is executed, A$ will be "JONES", and R will contain 452. The constants contained in a DATA statement are assigned in the order in which they are coded.

Any number of DATA statements may be included in a BASIC program. They may be placed anywhere in the program. When a BASIC program is run, the first thing that happens is that all the DATA statements are grouped together, and a single

Fig. 6.11: *The examination scoring program with READ/DATA statements.*

```
 10                              REM * PROGRAM TO COMPUTE SAT SCORES FOR A
 20                              REM * NUMBER OF STUDENTS
 30                              REM *    WRITTEN BY: W.S.DAVIS
 40                              REM *           1/10/81
 50                              REM * * * * * * * * * * * * * * * * * *
 60                              REM * THE FIRST STEP IS TO FILL A TABLE
 70                              REM * WITH STUDENT RAW SCORES.
 80 DIM R[25]
 90 FOR N=1 TO 25
100    READ R[N]
110 NEXT N
120                              REM * NOW, WE COMPUTE THE AVERAGE RAW SCORE
130 LET A=0
140 FOR N=1 TO 25
150    LET A=A+R[N]
160 NEXT N
170 LET M=A/25
180                              REM * GIVEN THE RAW SCORES AND THE COMPUTED
190                              REM * AVERAGE RAW SCORE, THE STUDENT'S SAT
200                              REM * CAN BE COMPUTED FROM THE FORMULA
210                              REM *    SAT = (RAW / AVG RAW) * 500
220                              REM * USING THIS FORMULA,THE AVERAGE SCORE
230                              REM * WILL BE 500. ADDITIONAL TESTS WILL BE
240                              REM * USED TO ENSURE THAT THE MAXIMUM SAT
250                              REM * SCORE WILL BE 800,AND THE MINIMUM
260                              REM * WILL BE 200. THE FINAL SCORE WILL BE
270                              REM * SHOWN TO ITS NEAREST INTEGER VALUE.
280                              REM *
290 PRINT TAB(10),"STUDENT";TAB(20),"RAW SCORE";TAB(30),"SAT SCORE"
300 FOR N=1 TO 25
310    LET S=(R[N]/M)*500
320    IF S<=800 THEN 350
330    LET S=800
340    GOTO 370
350    IF S>=200 THEN 370
360    LET S=200
370    LET S=INT(S)
380    PRINT TAB(13),N;TAB(23),R[N];TAB(33),S
390 NEXT N
400 STOP
900 DATA 73,92,85,104,98
910 DATA 106,50,44,90,80
920 DATA 75,78,83,91,58
930 DATA 125,36,170,12,42
940 DATA 92,82,72,62,52
999 END
```

string of constants is formed. The constants from the first (lowest numbered) DATA statement come first, and those in the last DATA statement come last. Values are then assigned from this string in response to READ statements.

Although it may be legal to place DATA statements anywhere in a program, it is not necessarily good programming form. A DATA statement is not executed; that is, it does not add, subtract, multiply, divide, compare, or request input or output. In fact, DATA statements tend to "get in the way", making a program more difficult to follow. In Fig. 6.11, all the DATA statements have been grouped at the end of the program (statement numbers 900 through 940). Here, they do not interfere with the logical flow of the program. Later, when the time comes to remove the READ/DATA statements and reinsert the INPUT statement, they can easily be found and removed.

When an INPUT statement is used, data is provided one value at a time, *after* the program begins to run. When READ and DATA statements are used, all the data values must be provided *before* the program begins to run. This is the essential difference between the INPUT statement and the READ statement.

What advantages are gained by using READ/DATA statements during testing? It is not necessary to retype the data values each time a test is run, which saves time.

Why not use the READ/DATA statements all the time? Most real programs are designed to be run more than once, usually with different data each time. If READ/DATA statements are used, the program must be changed each time it is run. If INPUT statements are used, the data can be changed without changing the program. The INPUT statement is more flexible.

THE PROGRAM WITHOUT ARRAYS: THE RESTORE STATEMENT

It is possible to write the examination scoring program without using an array. We needed an array to hold data in main memory so that we could use it again. A DATA statement defines a string of constants in main memory; the data is already there, so the array really is unnecessary.

It is easy to see how a READ statement in a loop can access twenty-five values (or any number of values) of a statistic such as raw score, with a subsequent instruction in the loop accumulating these values. Once the program has gone through the entire string, however, we want to go back and start over again with the first value as the "compute and print" loop begins. This can be done by coding a **RESTORE** statement:

```
statement no.    RESTORE
```

The RESTORE statement causes the system to "back up" in the string of constants created by DATA statements. By coding:

180 RESTORE

the program moves back to the beginning of the data string. Thus the first variable associated with the next READ statement will be assigned the very first value in the string. By coding:

220   RESTORE   910

the program moves back to the first constant defined in statement number 910. The use of a statement number is not legal in all versions of BASIC.

If the combination of instructions READ/DATA/RESTORE were used in solving the examination scoring problem, a first loop could read, in turn, each of the raw score values and accumulate them. After the average had been computed, a RESTORE statement would be used to set the data string counter back to the beginning of the string. The final loop would READ each of the values again, one at a time, and compute the score. A listing of this program is shown as Fig. 6.12.

READ/DATA VS. INPUT

A combination of READ and DATA statements can be used anytime an INPUT statement can be used. Which is better? Although specific cases might be cited favoring either, it is basically a matter of personal preference. A few general guidelines can, however, be established.

The READ/DATA combination is excellent during program testing, as it is not necessary to keep retyping the data each time a test is run. Clearly, if large amounts of data must be typed into the program, the "before the fact" nature of the DATA statements does tend to minimize typing errors. With large amounts of data, the fact that INPUT statements require the entry of data elements one at a time tends to slow down the program; the use of DATA statements tends to produce results more quickly. In some applications, it is highly desirable that input data not appear between lines of output on the terminal; using the READ/DATA combination tends to avoid this problem. On the negative side, alphanumeric constants must be enclosed in quote marks when using DATA statements; this is not necessary with INPUT statements.

The big advantage of the INPUT statement is its flexibility. New data can be processed without modifying the program. The data need not be known ahead of time. Using INPUT statements, it is possible to design a program that is almost conversational in nature, with data being provided by even an untrained terminal operator in response to English language questions. In "real world" computer programs, this flexibility is extremely valuable.

SUMMARY

In this chapter, we developed a program to compute scores on a standardized test modelled after the Scholastic Aptitude Test. The key problem arose from the fact that the data, raw scores, was used twice, once to compute the average raw score and again to compute the individual examination scores.

Fig. 6.12: *The examination grading program without arrays.*

```
 10                              REM * PROGRAM TO COMPUTE SAT SCORES FOR A
 20                              REM * NUMBER OF STUDENTS
 30                              REM *    WRITTEN BY: W.S.DAVIS
 40                              REM *             1/10/81
 50                              REM * * * * * * * * * * * * * * * * * * *
 60                              REM * THE FIRST STEP IS TO READ THE RAW
 70                              REM * SCORES, SUM THEM, AND COMPUTE THE
 80                              REM * AVERAGE RAW SCORE.
 90 LET A=0
100 FOR N=1 TO 25
110   READ R
120   LET A=A+R
130 NEXT N
140 LET M=A/25
150                             REM * THE DATA IS RESTORED; THUS THE NEXT
160                             REM * READ STATEMENT WILL REFER TO THE
170                             REM * FIRST RAW SCORE.
180 RESTORE
190                             REM * GIVEN THE RAW SCORES AND THE COMPUTED
200                             REM * AVERAGE RAW SCORE, THE STUDENT'S SAT
210                             REM * CAN BE COMPUTED FROM THE FORMULA
220                             REM *    SAT = (RAW / AVG RAW) * 500
230                             REM * USING THIS FORMULA,THE AVERAGE SCORE
240                             REM * WILL BE 500. ADDITIONAL TESTS WILL BE
250                             REM * USED TO ENSURE THAT THE MAXIMUM SAT
260                             REM * SCORE WILL BE 800,AND THE MINIMUM
270                             REM * WILL BE 200. THE FINAL SCORE WILL BE
280                             REM * SHOWN TO ITS NEAREST INTEGER VALUE.
290                             REM *
300 PRINT TAB(10),"STUDENT";TAB(20),"RAW SCORE";TAB(30),"SAT SCORE"
310 FOR N=1 TO 25
320   READ R
330   LET S=(R/M)*500
340   IF S<=800 THEN 370
350   LET S=800
360   GOTO 390
370   IF S>=200 THEN 390
380   LET S=200
390   LET S=INT(S)
400   PRINT TAB(13),N;TAB(23),R;TAB(33),S
410 NEXT N
420 STOP
900 DATA 123,114,95,83,75
910 DATA 72,68,69,93,35
920 DATA 2,170,75,65,43
930 DATA 28,68,78,82,95
940 DATA 105,98,88,77,66
999 END
```

To solve the program of multiple use of the data, we defined an array by using a DIM statement. An array is a series of related main memory locations. By using subscripts, the elements contained in the array can be uniquely identified.

We identified three primary functions the program would have to perform: fill the array, compute the average, and compute the individual scores. We then wrote the code for each function independently, putting the pieces together after defining the logic—a modular approach to programming.

As an aid to program testing, the READ/DATA statements were introduced. Later, by adding a RESTORE statement, we saw how the examination scoring program could be written without an array.

EXERCISES

1. Generalize the text example so that it accepts any number (up to a limit of 50) of raw scores and computes and prints the associated examination scores.

2. Add to the text example the logic needed to input the student's name and, later, to print the name along with the raw score and the examination score. Note: if character arrays are illegal on your system, you may not be able to do this. Use a student number instead.

3. In a different standarized test, the algorithm for computing a score begins with the computation of an average raw score. However, the final scores are to be generated with an average of 18, a maximum of 30, and a minimum of 0. Write a program to read the raw scores and compute individual examination scores using this new algorithm.

4. Write a program to generate a multiplication table. Use an array of ten elements to set up a series of computations in main memory (5*1, 5*2, 5*3, and so on, for example). Then copy the array to the terminal. In the next loop, compute the multiplication table for the next integer (the 6-times table, for example), and print it.

After you have completed this program, look into the use of 2-dimensional arrays on your system. Revise the program to set up a *complete* multiplication table in memory (1-times through 10-times) before printing or displaying the table.

5. Revise the wind chill factor program of Chapter 4. Set up an array of five elements to hold the computed wind chill factors for a constant temperature and for wind velocities ranging from 10 to 50 miles per hour. Print all five values on a single line. The objective is to print a table, with the wind velocity going across the top and the temperature going down the side, such as:

WIND VELOCITY-MPH

TEMP	10	20	30	40	50
-30	—	—	—	—	—
-20	—	—	—	—	—

and so on.

6.   Use arrays to generate a similar table (to the one described in exercise 5) for the temperature/humidity index described in Chapter 4, exercise 17.

7.   Write a program to read ten or more values (in random order) into an array. Search the array and find the largest value. Search the array again and find the smallest value. Print the largest value, the smallest value, and their difference.

8.   If character arrays are legal on your computer's version of BASIC, revise exercise 7 to fill and search a character array.

9.   An automobile dealership employs ten salespeople. Each year, a competition is held. The employee who sells the most cars is identified, as is the employee who sells the fewest cars. The high salesperson is paid a bonus of $10 for the difference between his or her sales and those of the low salesperson. The low salesperson is assigned to the used car lot for the next year. Sales statistics by month for the past year were as follows:

Person	J	F	M	A	M	J	J	A	S	O	N	D
1	12	7	7	4	4	0	9	5	0	9	4	6
2	0	9	2	11	0	5	3	9	4	5	5	7
3	5	1	6	6	8	7	8	0	5	12	6	5
4	3	10	15	6	1	9	6	3	4	9	5	3
5	4	7	7	5	7	4	15	2	5	3	1	9
6	9	2	2	5	3	5	12	16	13	0	5	5
7	8	0	6	8	9	3	6	2	3	1	7	5
8	8	0	0	5	4	9	4	2	2	7	8	2
9	8	2	4	2	8	3	3	2	0	6	8	5
10	6	5	7	4	9	8	0	8	6	3	7	6

HINT: define one DATA statement for each salesperson. Set up an array. READ the sales statistics and accumulate the monthly sales for each salesperson; place these accumulated totals in the array. Look at exercise 7 for a hint as to how to continue.

10. Read at least ten values into an array. The input data should be in random order. Sort it.

11. Two common statistical computations are the mean and standard deviation of a set of data points. If we call our data points:

$$X_1, X_2, X_3, \ldots x_n$$

the mean can be defined as:

$$\overline{X} = \frac{\sum_{i=1}^{n} X_i}{n}$$

or: X-bar is equal to the sum of all the individual values of X divided by the number of different values. Standard deviation is defined as:

$$s = \sqrt{\frac{\sum_{i=1}^{n} (X_i - \overline{X})^2}{n - 1}}$$

In English this means:

   a. Subtract the computed mean $(\overline{X})$ from each individual value of X and square the result.

   b. Sum these individual results for all values of X.

   c. Divide this sum by n, the number of values, minus 1.

   d. Take the square root of this result.

Write a program to compute these two statistics from input data consisting of at least 10 data points.

12. At some point in your education, an instructor has undoubtedly shown you a frequency distribution of grades something like the following:

Grade Range	Number of students
90 and above	5
80-89	8
70-79	12
60-69	8
59 and below	5

By so grouping the data, the instructor (not to mention the student) gets a very clear picture of where each student stands with respect to the rest of the class. The use of frequency distributions is not, of course, limited to the field of education, being commonly used in business, government and other fields to group and clarify such data as: salary levels, order status, product quality, production rate, sales results, population statistics, and many other types of data too numerous to mention.

The field of statistics uses several terms to describe a frequency distribution. In the sample distribution shown above, we have five *classes*: 90 and above, 80-89, 70-79, 60-69, and 59 and below; each class is a single logical grouping of data. The *class interval* is ten; i.e., each class contains ten possible values. The *class limits* are 90 and below 60; these represent the initial value of the top and bottom "open ended" classes.

Other arrangements are possible. Let's say, for example, we were to specify an *upper* class limit of 95, a class internal of 5, and a total of 11 classes. The resulting classes would be:

```
95 and above
90-94
85-89
80-84
75-79
70-74
65-69
60-64
55-59
50-54
49 and below
```

Write a program to generate a frequency distribution. Your program should INPUT the upper (or lower) class limit, the class interval, and the number of classes. Run the program at least twice, using different frequency distribution parameters. Use DATA statements for the test data (except for the parameters).

13. Sales records for the past month show that our three salespeople sold the following amounts of our four basic products:

Product

		A	B	C	D
	1	14	24	3	57
Salesperson	2	7	17	8	35
	3	22	20	5	32

Product selling prices are:

Product	Unit Price
A	$10.50
B	$15.55
C	$25.00
D	$ 5.95

Write a program to read each salesperson's record and print a sales report consisting of the following information:

SALESPERSON	PRODUCT A		PRODUCT B		PRODUCT C		PRODUCT D		TOTAL
	QUANTITY	REVENUE	QUANTITY	REVENUE	QUANTITY	REVENUE	QUANTITY	REVENUE	REVENUE

Revenue is defined as the product of quantity and unit price. Use one DATA statement for each salesperson's record. Use one or more arrays to hold the sales statistics.

14. A speciality shop stocks ten items. The current stock on hand for each of the ten items is as follows:

Item No.	Quantity	Item No.	Quantity
1	14	6	37
2	28	7	18
3	3	8	9
4	95	9	42
5	12	10	11

During the current week, all part numbers had activity as follows:

DAY	ITEM	CODE	QUANT.	DAY	ITEM	CODE	QUANT.
M	2	2	5	W	7	2	8
M	5	2	10	T	3	2	12
M	9	2	23	T	6	2	10
T	2	2	15	T	8	2	20
T	1	2	10	F	1	1	25
T	4	2	15	F	10	2	3
T	5	2	2	F	4	2	32
W	8	1	25	F	6	2	10
W	7	2	8	F	7	1	25
W	3	1	25				

Each transaction should be represented by a separate DATA statement, with a code of "1" meaning an addition to inventory, and a code of "2" meaning a deletion from inventory.

Initialize an array to hold the current level of inventory for each item; INPUT the complete "old inventory" at the start of your program. Read individual transactions, keeping track of additions and deletions by item number. HINT: Use the item number as your subscript.

Print a report showing: Beginning inventory, the sum of all additions to inventory, the sum of all deletions from inventory, and ending inventory. Place an asterisk (*) to the right of the ending inventory field for any part number having an ending inventory less than ten (10)—this is a reorder flag. Use explicit column headings.

15. READ a series of grades (in random order) ranging from a low of 40 to a high of 100 into an array (use DATA statements for the grades). Count the number of grades in the 90s, the 80s, the 70s, the 60s, and below 60. Print the counts.

16.   Add to the payroll program of Chapter 5 a new subroutine to compute the amount of local tax due. Local tax varies with the employee's place of residence. We have defined the following city codes and associated percentage rates:

CITY	RATE
1	1.5%
2	1.0%
3	0.5%
4	0.75%
5	0.25%
6	1.25%

At the start of your program, link to a new subroutine that fills a local tax rate array from a DATA statement containing these percentages. Within the mainline of your program, include a variable for city code as part of your INPUT statement. Link to a new subroutine that searches the table by the city code and computes local tax (a percentage of gross pay).

17.   An earlier exercise, number 12, asked you to write a program to generate a frequency distribution. Your output consisted of a series of numbers, one for each class.

Modify the program to print a bar chart of the distribution. For example, the sample data in exercise 12 was

Grade range	Number of students
90 and above	5
80-89	8
70-79	12
60-69	8
below 60	5

A bar chart for this distribution would be:

Grade range	Distribution
90 and above	*****
80-89	*******
70-79	***********
60-69	*******
below 60	*****

Module C

More on Arrays

The skilled programmer can do a great deal with arrays. In business programming, various tables can be set up and used. In computational or scientific programming, the rules of linear algebra can be used to manipulate arrays. If you become serious about programming, you will almost certainly find yourself using arrays. This module presents a bit more detail on BASIC arrays.

141

A FEW CODING RULES

1. Always code your DIM statements *before* referencing an element in the array. In fact, it is a good idea to code all your DIM statements at the beginning of the program, following your REM statements and preceeding any executable code.

2. Although most versions of BASIC allow the programmer to use any valid variable name as an array name, some restrict you to a single letter only; on such systems, for example, A3 would be an illegal array name. Check the reference manual for the rule on your system.

3. Do not use the same name for both an array *and* a regular variable. Such use is illegal on many systems. Even if your systems allows you to refer to A(1) and A in the same program, don't; it can lead to very confusing code.

4. The lower bound on subscripts is 1 on most systems. A few allow the programmer to refer to A(0), but this is the exception rather than the rule.

5. Subscripts should be positive integers. BASIC will, in most cases, convert any value or expression you supply to the nearest integer, and then use the integer (whole number) value as the subscript. The results, however, are often unpredictable. For example, if I $= 4$, what is the element defined by X(I/3)? Does the element change if I $= 5$? To avoid confusion, it is recommended that you use the INT function to control the value of the subscript; for example, X(INT(I/3)). Using the INT function puts you in control.

6. Avoid "out-of-bounds" subscripts. For example, the element X(15) does not exist in an array of 10 elements, nor does the element X(-1). Most versions of BASIC will terminate your program when such conditions are encountered. A few do not, generating unpredictable results. If there is a chance that a subscript will go out of bounds as the result of a computation, test the subscript before using it.

7. A few versions of BASIC preset the value of each array element, usually to zero. Most do not. Don't assume anything. Even if your system presets array values, code the instructions to initialize the array. It is simply bad coding practice not to.

8. A few versions of BASIC will assume the size of an array if you fail to code a DIM statement. Once again, failing to code DIM statements is bad coding practice.

9. Occasionally, you will encounter a need to code an array without knowing exactly how many elements will be in the array. You will be tempted to code something like DIM X(N). Don't! In most versions of BASIC, you *must* specify the number of elements in the array.

STRING ARRAYS

String arrays are not available on some systems. When they are available, they are defined much like a numeric array. For example:

```
30   DIM   T$ (25)
```

defines a string array of twenty-five elements. Subscripts are used to refer to specific elements in a string array; the rules for defining subscripts are the same as in other arrays.

In some versions of BASIC, a string array is used to set the length of a string variable. Under such systems, the variable A$ defines sufficient space to hold a single character only. By coding:

```
50   DIM   A$ (16)
```

space is set aside to hold a 16-character field. Subscripts can then be used to manipulate the individual characters in this field.

EXERCISES:

1.   Imagine that your instructor has decided to use the computer to keep track of your course grades for the current term. For each student in the class, the following information is to be stored: identification number, name, first exam grade, second exam grade, third exam grade, final exam grade, and homework grade. One array is to be set up for each data item. Write the BASIC code needed to initialize each array. How many elements will be in each array? Which arrays will be string and which numeric? Can you possibly initialize all elements in all arrays now? Set any field that is unknown at the beginning of the term to zero.

MULTI-DIMENSIONAL ARRAYS

Many versions of BASIC support the use of two- and three-dimensional arrays. For example, the DIM statement:

```
40   DIM   A(5,5)
```

would create an array of 5 rows and 5 columns; a representation of this array is shown as Fig. C.1. Note that there are 25 elements in the array; each of the 5 rows contains 5 columns. Each element in the array is defined by two subscripts; for example, the element at the top left is A(1,1), while the one in the middle of the array is A(3,3). Any number of rows and columns may be coded (up to the limit imposed by your system, of course). For example, the statement:

```
70   DIM   X(2,4)
```

would define an array of eight elements.

A three-dimensional array is one that has three subscripts. For example, the statement:

A(1,1)	A(1,2)	A(1,3)	A(1,4)	A(1,5)
A(2,1)	A(2,2)	A(2,3)	A(2,4)	A(2,5)
A(3,1)	A(3,2)	A(3,3)	A(3,4)	A(3,5)
A(4,1)	A(4,2)	A(4,3)	A(4,4)	A(4,5)
A(5,1)	A(5,2)	A(5,3)	A(5,4)	A(5,5)

```
50   DIM   R(2,3,4)
```

would create a "2 by 3 by 4" array, giving a total of 24 elements. The rules for coding subscripts are the same as they were in single-dimensional arrays.

THE MAT FUNCTIONS

By using multi-dimensional arrays, the BASIC programmer can, on many systems, take advantage of a number of excellent matrix manipulation functions. Many of these functions are based on the standard rules of linear algebra. It is not our intent to introduce the rules of linear algebra; your instructor or another course is assumed to be the source of that information.

Before we list the various MAT functions, one point must be made. Consider the following three arrays:

DIM X(5)   DIM X(1,5)   DIM X(5,1)

Technically, all three are identical—they all generate exactly five elements. The MAT functions on your computer may, however, treat them differently. Check the reference manual, or experiment on your own.

The following MAT functions are available on many (though not all) versions of BASIC. The rules of linear algebra must be followed in determining the proper dimensions for result and intermediate arrays (or matrices).

Function	Description
MAT A=B	Simple assignment of matrix A to matrix B. Both must have same dimensions.
MAT A=B+C	Add arrays A and B, and place the sum in array A.
MAT A=B-C	Subtract array C from array B and place the difference in array A.
MAT A=B*C	Multiply matrix B by matrix C using the rules of matrix algebra. The product is placed in matrix A.
MAT A=(m)*C	Multiply each of the elements in matrix C by the scalar (non-matrix) expression represented by (m) and place the product in matrix A. Note that the scalar should be enclosed in parentheses.
MAT A=IDN	Initializes an identity matrix.
MAT A=ZER	Sets each element in matrix A to zero.
MAT A=CON	Set each element in matrix A to 1.
MAT A=TRN(B)	Transposes matrix B and places the result in matrix A.
MAT A=INV(B)	Inverts matrix B and places the result in matrix A. Both A and B must be square matrices.
MAT A=DET(B)	Finds the determinate of matrix B and places the result in A, a regular variable. B must be a square matrix.
MAT INPUT A	Obtains values for each of the elements in an array from the terminal, usually in row/column order.
MAT READ A	Obtains values for each of the elements in an array from DATA statements, usually in row/column order.
MAT PRINT A	Prints or displays the current value of each of the elements in an array, usually in row/column order.

What Next?

7

BASIC: GETTING STARTED

This is a book on the BASIC language. The title is *BASIC: Getting Started*. The title very clearly describes the book's intent: to help you get started as a programmer.

Assuming that you have read carefully, assuming (more importantly) that you have written a number of programs, you now know how to program. You have learned a valuable skill. As is the case with any skill, however, "practice makes perfect". You are still a novice. The only way to *really* learn how to program *is* to program. No matter what your field of major study, no matter what your job may be, computer programming can be an invaluable tool. But it's all up to you. If you use your skill, you will get better. If you choose not to use it, you will probably lose it.

As you begin to write more and more significant programs, you will eventually have a need for features of the BASIC language that were not covered here. Where do you find information on these features? In a reference manual; you should be able to find a copy somewhere in or near your computer center. Reference manuals are not written for beginners; they are written for people who already know how to program. Reference manuals describe, in detail, precisely how specific instructions work. If you cannot figure out what instruction should be coded next, the reference manual will not help you, if you *know* what instruction should be coded next, the reference manual will show you how to code it. You know how to program. You can read the reference manual. Learn to use it. Of course, there are other sources of programming information—other programmers. Ask. Most programmers are only too happy to show a novice a few tricks.

147

But the bottom line remains: the only way to learn to program *is* to program. Do it. That's how you will learn.

SOME POINTERS

There are a few BASIC features that you will almost certainly encounter as your skill increases. Consider, for example, output. Perhaps you have already felt a sense of dissatisfaction with the way the printed output from a BASIC program looks. Columns of figures are not always nicely aligned; the spacing of related fields seems, at times, almost whimsical. With only semicolons and the TAB function to control spacing, a solution is difficult to imagine. Most versions of *extended* BASIC include a PRINT USING or PRINT under mask statement which allows for precise, character by character control of the output line. Check it out in the reference manual.

If your interest is science or mathematics, you will eventually encounter a problem that calls for the manipulation of matrices. Many versions of BASIC, especially extended BASIC, include excellent (and easy to use) matrix operators. Look them up under MAT. The scientific programmer may also be interested in using library programs that perform common statistical and mathematical computations—if someone else has already written the program, why "reinvent the wheel"? Ask an experienced programmer or the person in charge of your computer center; many of these library programs are excellent.

If you are a business major or if you hold a job in the world of business, you may not be quite so interested in the scientific features of BASIC. Typical business computer applications include payroll, accounts receivable, accounts payable, general ledger, and several other accounting-oriented tasks. Such applications are characterized by a great deal of input and output—in other words, a large amount of data. To handle such quantities of data, the programmer often finds it necessary to define a number of *files* on inexpensive secondary storage media such as magnetic tape or disk. The procedures for creating and accessing files vary significantly among the many different versions of BASIC. Study the reference manual carefully.

It's up to you.

Answers to Selected Exercises

MODULE A, page 41.

1. a. correct.
    b. correct.
    c. incorrect. Blank space between 5 and 1.
    d. incorrect. Comma illegal.
    e. incorrect. Too many digits. This number would probably be accepted and stored as 123456.0. Note that on some systems this constant would be legal.
    f. correct.
    g. correct.
    h. correct.
    i. incorrect. Exponent too large. Note that on some systems this constant would be legal.
    j. correct.
    k. correct.
    l. correct. The number in normalized form would be 0.123456   E38.

2. a. 3.14159.
    b. 0.3937 inch/centimeter or 2.54 centimeter/inch.
    c. 39.37 inches/meter.
    d. 0.6214 miles/kilometer or 1.6093 kilometers/mile.
    e. At most schools, 4.000.
    f. Varies. Typically about 64 semester credits for an associate degree and 128 for a bachelor's degree.
    g. Just over 200,000,000, which, in BASIC, is best written as 2.0   E8.
    h. This one may be difficult to find. The basic idea is that an atom is very small, and its size is best written as a floating-point number with a negative exponent, such as 10^{-10} meters or 10^{-8} centimeters.
    i. Alpha Centari is 4.3 light years away.
    j. 5.8657   E12 miles/light year.
    k. A typical FM station would be 100 megahertz or 100   E6 hertz. A typical AM station would be 700 kilohertz or 700   E3 hertz.
    l. Probably something like 4.25. Why have we not coded a dollar sign?
    m. About 5000.00
    n. 33.3333 RPM is as close as we can get.

MODULE A, page 42.

1. a. legal.
   b. illegal. Too many characters. Also, two alphabetic characters.
   c. legal.
   d. illegal. Letter must come first.
   e. legal.
   f. legal.
   g. illegal. Too many characters. Also, two digits.
   h. legal.
   i. legal. (But not very good, as it is often difficult to tell the difference between the letter O and the digit zero by sight.)
   j. illegal. Two letters.
   k. illegal. Two letters. The fact that a capital I is sometimes used to represent the digit one is beside the point.
   l. illegal. Cannot use lower case letter.

MODULE A, page 45.

1. a. $X + Y + (2 * Z) + 8$ Note: parentheses not required.
   b. $(2 * A) + (4 * B) + (4 * C) - (2 * D)$ Note: parentheses not required.
   c. $(X + Y) / (A + B)$ Note: parentheses *are* needed here. Why?
   d. $((- B) + (B \uparrow 2 - 4 * A * C) \uparrow 0.5) / (2 * A)$ Note: parentheses *are* needed. Why?
   e. $(X * Y) - (2 * (X \uparrow 2) * (Y \uparrow 2)) + (3 * (X \uparrow 3) * Y \uparrow 3))$ Are these parentheses needed? Why, or why not?
   f. $(A / 3) + (B \uparrow 2) / 4 - (C \uparrow 3) / 3$
   g. $(A * B * C * D) / (W * X * Y * Z) + 18.5$

2. a. $0.5 * B * H$ [B = base; H = height]
   b. $X \uparrow 3$ [X = length of one side]
   c. $3.1416 * (R \uparrow 3)$ [R = radius]
   d. $3.1416 * (R \uparrow 2) * H$ [R = radius; H = height]
   e. H / B [H = hits; B = times at bat]
   f. $R / (I / 9)$ [R = runs; I = innings]
   g. P / C [P = grade points; C = credits]
   h. $B * 0.05$ [B = old balance]

3. a. 4.5
   b. 7.5
   c. 2
   d. 2
   e. 3
   f. 12
   g. 36
   h. 81
   i. 6
   j. 0.75

1. "W. S. DAVIS"
   "MIAMI UNIVERSITY, DEPT. OF SYSTEMS ANALYSIS"
   "OXFORD, OHIO"
   "45056"
   "(513) 529-2338"

2. "123-45-6789" or simply "123456789"
   In the first case, the dash is illegal in a numeric field. Even without the dash, there are simply too many characters for most versions of BASIC.

BASIC Instruction
Quick Reference

Use the following index to quickly find the page where a given BASIC instruction is explained.